*Law*Basics

TRUSTS

Other titles in the Series

Agency
Commercial Law
Constitutional Law
Contract Law
Evidence
Scottish Legal System
Succession

AUSTRALIA
LBC Information Services
Sydney

CANADA AND THE USA
Carswell
Toronto

NEW ZEALAND
Brooker's
Auckland

*Law*Basics

TRUSTS

By

Roderick R. M. Paisley, Ph.D., LL.B. Dip.L.P., N.P.

Lecturer in Law,
University of Aberdeen

EDINBURGH
W. GREEN/Sweet & Maxwell
1999

First published 1999
Reprinted 2003

Published in 1998 by W. Green & Son Limited of
21 Alva Street,
Edinburgh, EH2 4PS

Typeset by Trinity Typesetting,
Edinburgh

Printed in Great Britain by Creative Print & Design
Wales, Ebbw Vale

No natural forests were destroyed to make this product;
only farmed timber was used and replanted.

A CIP catalogue record of this book is available from the British Library.

ISBN 0 414 01330 1

For Debbie, Victoria and Robert

PREFACE

The aim of this book is to give an overview of the law of trusts in Scotland. It is intended to encourage readers to look further at this interesting field of law.

Many colleagues and friends have assisted and made helpful comments on earlier drafts of the manuscript. Particular thanks are due to Professors Douglas Cusine and Michael Meston, Dr Iain MacNeil and Alison MacNeil, William Craig, Judith Pearson, Scott Styles and Clive Phillips.

CONTENTS

CONTENTS

TABLE OF CASES

1. INTRODUCTORY CONCEPTS

INTRODUCTION

The word "trust" in Scots law can mean several things. For the purpose of this book the word indicates a situation where property is vested in a party known as a "trustee" to be administered on behalf of other parties known as "beneficiaries" for certain purposes. The party who sets up such an arrangement and who specifies the purposes of the trust is known as the "truster" or "settlor". A simple example of a trust is where a man conveys his house to his solicitor in trust for the purposes of providing a home for his wife and children.

There is a statutory definition of the terms "trust" and "trustee" in the Trusts (Scotland) Act 1921, s.2. These are definitions for the purposes of the legislation but they cover most arrangements regarded as trusts and parties regarded as trustees at common law.

In any trust the essentials are threefold as follows:

(a) the existence of the parties — truster, trustee and beneficiary;
(b) the transfer of property to the trustees; and
(c) the laying down of purposes for the trust.

A trust is a "fiduciary" relationship. This means that it is founded upon good faith and this has significant effects on the relationship of the parties to the trust *inter se*.

HISTORICAL BACKGROUND AND SOURCES OF LAW

In the law of trusts Scots law has benefited from the importation of ideas from Roman law and English law but has developed along unique lines. The law of trusts in Scotland is different from the law of trusts in England in many material points although Scotland has borrowed a number of English concepts and some terminology relative to trusts. For example, the terms "settlor", "resulting trust", "*cy-près*" and "constructive trust" originate in England. The importation of English concepts is an ongoing process. Nevertheless, in a brief overview of Scottish trusts one should, for the most part, ignore English law.

There remain many important differences between the English and Scottish laws of trusts. For example:

(a) the beneficiary in a Scottish trust has no real right or separate interest in the trust property, whereas in England the beneficiary is regarded as having a "beneficial interest" in the trust property;
(b) the distinction between private and public trusts in Scots law is not the same as with the English division between private and charitable trusts;

(c) alimentary liferents are recognised by the law of Scotland but are unknown in England;

(d) the law of England makes much greater use of the device of constructive trust to provide augmented proprietorial remedies where other existing remedies are regarded as inadequate;

(e) English law requires all trustees to act in the administration of a trust but Scots law allows decisions to be made by majority vote;

(f) the Scottish courts do not possess the same wide powers as are enjoyed by their English counterparts in relation to the authorisation of acts of administration that are expedient for the trust; and

(g) the English courts may sanction an act by a trustee which would otherwise be regarded as improper on the basis that the trustee acted as *auctor in rem suam*, but the Scottish courts do not have this power.

ESSENTIALS OF TRUSTS — THE PARTIES

A trust, at least initially, involves a tripartite relationship. In any trust three parties must be involved — the truster, the trustee and the beneficiary.

These three parties need not be totally distinct persons — the same individual may appear in more than one capacity. A truster may also be a trustee. A truster or trustee may also be a beneficiary subject to the qualification that a trustee cannot be the sole beneficiary. If a single individual with the real right in the property (a sole trustee) becomes the person who alone has a personal right against the trustee (a sole beneficiary) the trust is extinguished by the doctrine of confusion and that person becomes the owner of the property free from the trust (McLaren, *Wills and Succession*, para. 1512).

There may be more than one truster, more than one trustee and more than one beneficiary.

NUMBER OF TRUSTEES

The general rule that a truster is free to require that there be one or more trustees as he sees fit is subject to a number of qualifications.

It is unwise for a truster to specify in a trust deed that there shall be only one trustee at any one time. Such a situation is best avoided at least where the sole trustee is a natural person. Problems may arise upon the death of a sole trustee. (See pp. 19 and 25).

Certain statutes provide for a maximum number of trustees. In the context of the law of bankruptcy only one permanent trustee may be elected in a particular sequestration at any one time (Bankruptcy (Scotland) Act 1985, s.3).

There are certain statutory provisions providing for a minimum number of trustees in trusts subject to special taxation rules. For example, in relation to public trusts with charitable purposes, the Lord Advocate and the trustees have power to ensure that there are at least three trustees notwithstanding any provision in the trust deed to the contrary (Law Reform (Miscellaneous Provisions) (Scotland) Act 1990, s. 13).

CONTEMPORANEOUS EXISTENCE OF VARIOUS PARTIES

In many cases in relation to trusts, the three parties to a trust, the truster, the trustee and the beneficiary will exist at the same time. A simple example is an *inter vivos* trust where a man sets up a trust for the benefit of his children with his wife acting as the trustee.

Contemporaneous existence of all the parties, however, is not an absolute requirement. For example, in relation to a *mortis causa* trust, the trust does not come into existence until after the death of the truster. Similarly in relation to an *inter vivos* trust the death of the truster does not bring the trust to an end. In relation to this last point one may note a point of distinction between trusts and mandate, deposit or agency. These three relationships come to an end respectively with the death of the mandant, depositee or the principal.

The beneficiaries need not exist at the time of the creation of the trust. For example, a trust may be created for the benefit of persons as yet unborn whether they are children *in utero* (in the womb) or as yet unconceived. Nevertheless, where a trust is established for future children it will remain revocable by the truster until a child is born. This is illustrated by *Watt v. Watson* (1897). Here a woman created a trust for the purposes of payment of the income of the estate to herself and her husband and the holding of the fee for the children of the marriage. It was held that until such time as children were born to the marriage the woman (with the consent of the husband) could revoke the deed.

EXISTENCE OF BENEFICIARIES

For a trust to be valid there must be identifiable beneficiaries. In relation to private trusts these are usually specified individuals or legal bodies. In relation to public trusts, the beneficiaries will constitute a specified section of the general public and it will not be necessary to name each of the benefited individuals within that section of the public.

Exceptional cases exist in relation to trusts which are set up to benefit animals or to erect gravestones for a deceased truster. These sorts of trust may appear to run contrary to the principle that a trust purpose is valid only if it confers some beneficial interest in property on another living person. Nevertheless, both types of trust are recognised as valid in Scotland — provided in the case of gravestones that they are on a suitably modest scale conform to accepted custom in Scotland. According to one method of analysis, in such cases the beneficiaries are not the deceased party or the animals but the general public. For example, the purpose of the trust for animals may be regarded as the welfare of animals but it is the public in general who receive the benefit of having the animals looked after. Similarly, the purpose of the trust may be the erection of a gravestone but the public in general receive the benefit of having an appropriate degree of reverence and dignity accorded to the deceased.

ESSENTIALS OF TRUSTS — THE TRANSFER OF PROPERTY TO TRUSTEES

The existence of trust property and the passing of title to that property to the trustees is essential for any trust. In a trust the trustees have the real right in the property which is enforceable against the whole world including, in appropriate cases, the truster and the beneficiaries.

The vesting of the property right in the trustees distinguishes a trust from many other legal relationships. For example in the relationship of principal and agent the property is not vested in the agent.

In some cases there is a relationship known as a "trust for administration". This occurs where a person instructs another (the "trustee") to administer his property for the first party or another person. This phrase "trust for administration" may serve to confuse matters. Such a relationship is not really a trust at all because the truster is not divested of the property right and the "trustees" are not the owners of the trust property. An example of an administrative trust may occur where a person who recognises that he has limited commercial skill hands over his property to a bank to be administered for him. Another example is where a government minister who is likely to take decisions affecting his existing investments does not wish to sell his investments but wishes to avoid claims that he has acted with a conflict of interest. Whilst he is in office he may hand over his shares to be administered for him in a "blind trust" so that the decisions relevant to the investments are not taken by him personally.

ESSENTIALS OF TRUSTS — THE LAYING DOWN OF PURPOSES

A trust must have certain purposes.

Where the trust has been created by the voluntary act of the truster these purposes will be specified by him. Where the trust has been implied by law the purposes will also be implied by law. Where a trust has been expressly created by statute its purposes will frequently be set out in the statute in express terms. See, for example, the listing of the various functions of a permanent trustee on the estate of a sequestrated party in the Bankruptcy (Scotland) Act 1985, s. 3(1).

The essence of the rights of the beneficiaries is to insist that the trustees implement the trust purposes.

TRUSTS ARE NOT CORPORATIONS

Although a body corporate may be a trustee, a trust is not a corporation.

An entity created by statute may be called a "trust" or "trustees" and be a corporate body. See, *e.g.* National Health Service Trusts created under the National Health Service (Scotland) Act 1978, s. 12A and Church of Scotland General Trustees created under the Church of Scotland (General Trustees) Order Confirmation Act 1921.

2. THE COMMON USES OF TRUSTS

MODERN OCCURRENCE OF TRUSTS

There are specialised rules in relation to many of types of trusts. This text will not examine these special rules except as occasional illustrations of the variety of trusts. Nevertheless, the reader should be aware that trusts crop up frequently. For example, they are commonly encountered in relation to situations such as the following:

(a) investment and financial planning purposes, including pension funds, trusts for employee share ownership and unit trusts;
(b) protective purposes, including trusts for children, incapable persons such as mentally incapable individuals and persons of full capacity but limited ability; and
(c) commercial purposes, such as the manipulation of the control of companies by the ownership of shares by a trust.

Private trusts are frequently encountered in connection with taxation. This text will not deal with the rules of taxation relative to trusts. Nevertheless the reader should be aware that trusts are commonly employed for the purposes of fiscal efficiency and the retention of family wealth. Whether they will be effective to do so will depend on the taxation statutes in force from time to time. Broadly speaking, the benefit of the trust in the context of taxation is that it enables the separation of the legal ownership from the beneficial ownership. One should never create a private trust without first considering the tax implications.

COMMON INSTANCES OF MODERN TRUSTS

Five common situations where trusts occur and where there are many additional specialised rules are:

(a) executors;
(b) judicial factors;
(c) improper liferents;
(d) trustees in bankruptcy; and
(e) conveyancing matters.

Executors
Executors are trustees in respect of the executry estate of the deceased.

The deceased's estate, both heritable and moveable, vests, for the purposes of administration, in the executor by virtue of confirmation (Succession (Scotland) Act 1964, s. 14(1). It is the confirmation, not the appointment of the executor, which itself constitutes a valid title to heritage and may be used as a link in title.

The principal function or duty of the executor is to ingather and distribute the estate. Thus he should pay the funeral and testamentary expenses, the deceased's debts, the legacies and the residuary legatee or the persons entitled to the estate on intestacy as circumstances dictate. The executor is therefore said to be a debtor to the legatee or the heirs on intestacy (*per* Lord President Inglis in *Jamieson v. Clark* (1872)).

Judicial factors
Judicial factors are trustees appointed by the court in a variety of situations.

A judicial factor is an officer of the court appointed by the Court of Session acting under the *nobile officium* (residual discretionary power) or by the Court of Session or sheriff court under certain statutes.

Very broadly speaking, judicial factors are appointed to administer property in cases where the property is the subject of litigation or because it lacks some other competent administration at the date of the factor's appointment.

All judicial factors are under the supervision of the Accountant of Court. Judicial factors include parties such as *curators bonis* to insane persons, judicial factors on insolvent estates and judicial factors appointed on the estates of defaulting solicitors.

Improper liferents
Improper liferents (otherwise known as "trust" or "beneficiary" liferents) involve trustees who hold the property for the benefit of two distinct types of beneficiary, the liferenter and the fiar. By contrast, in a proper liferent there is no issue of trust and the liferenter has a real right which he may enforce against the whole of the world. The right of the liferenter in a proper liferent is more than a beneficial right and is a real right less extensive than the right of full property. In relation to a proper liferent, during the liferenter's lifetime, this lesser real right co-exists with the real right of *dominium* held by the fiar.

The interest of the liferenter is to enjoy the subjects for the term of the liferent. He is entitled to the income of the property. The fiar is entitled to the capital of the trust property. The interest of the fiar is (a) not to have the subjects diminished and (b) on the termination of the liferent to have the subjects conveyed to him. The fiar in this case is frequently also the trustee.

Liferents are extremely flexible particularly in relation to the discretion which may be afforded to trustees in relation to powers to advance capital to either the liferenter or the fiar. The flexibility may even extend to giving the trustees the right to determine who will take the capital at the termination of the liferent.

Improper liferents may be alimentary or non-alimentary.

Alimentary liferents
Although much less common than they were only 50 years ago, alimentary liferents are still to be found, especially in relation to provision in a will by a husband for his widow in respect of the matrimonial home. An alimentary liferent differs from an ordinary liferent in three main ways:

(1) An alimentary liferent is a special form of liferent in which property is given to trustees for the purpose of providing the liferenter with funds from which his maintenance and support is drawn or his education paid. A non-alimentary liferent may provide funds for the liferenter for much more than mere subsistence or maintenance. A liferent may lose its alimentary character if the underlying reason for its creation has ceased to exist. For example a liferent set up for the education of the beneficiary will cease to be alimentary when the beneficiary completes full-time education. It will then become an ordinary liferent which is capable of renunciation by the liferenter (see, *e.g.* *McMurdo's Trs v. McMurdo* (1897)).

(2) In so far as it is not excessive for the liferenter's maintenance at the level to which he is accustomed, an alimentary liferent is protected from creditors of the liferenter. Any excess will, however, be available to his creditors (see *Livingstone v. Livingstone* (1886)).

(3) Once the alimentary liferenter accepts the liferent, he cannot thereafter renounce or assign it. This is now modified by Trusts (Scotland) Act 1961, s. 1(4) which allows the court to authorise the variation or revocation of an alimentary liferent.

Trustees in bankruptcy

This is a specialised area of law with many detailed rules laid down in statute. The appointment of either the interim trustee or the permanent trustee and the powers afforded to both are dealt with in the Bankruptcy (Scotland) Act 1985.

Where a person becomes insolvent, the court may be requested to award sequestration of his estate. The party appointed to oversee this is the trustee in bankruptcy, who administers a bankrupt's estate for the benefit of creditors.

In the rare situation where there is property left over after paying off the creditors of the sequestrated party and the expenses of sequestration, the permanent trustee will hold this remaining property on a resulting trust for the debtor (Bankruptcy (Scotland) Act 1985, s. 51(5)).

Conveyancing matters

Trusts arise in the context of the conveyancing of heritable property in a number of situations. Some of the more common of these are as follows:

Frequently upon the settlement of a conveyancing transaction a minor matter cannot be finalised on the date of settlement. For example, when a purchaser buys a house there is a missing item such as a minute of waiver or a building warrant which simply cannot be produced at settlement but which is likely to turn up within a reasonable time. To enable settlement to occur the purchaser may be willing to hand over the bulk of the purchase price in exchange for all other settlement items and to place the balance in a bank account in trust for the seller and purchaser. This constitutes a trust for both parties. The money is paid over to the seller only if the missing item is produced. The documentation entered into at settlement usually provides that if the missing item is not produced within a certain time the money will be returned to the purchaser.

The opinion of Lord Jauncey sitting in the House of Lords in *Sharp v. Thomson* (1997) has caused much recent debate. The case concerned purchasers of a flat in Aberdeen who paid the price to the selling company but who did not record their disposition before a receiver was appointed to the company in terms of a pre-existing floating charge. A competition arose between the purchasers and the receiver. After much litigation it was eventually held that the purchasers had a better title than the receiver. The reasoning of the House of Lords is obscure but Lord Jauncey was of the view that upon delivery of the disposition the "beneficial interest" in the property passed to the purchasers and this took the property outwith the ambit of the floating charge. The concept of "beneficial ownership" in this context is a wholly novel creation by Lord Jauncey. It is unclear whether it would be the same as a beneficiary's right to trust property but that appears to be the nearest equivalent in Scotland. The substance and nature of the concept is so unclear that it is to be hoped that the opinion will not be followed in subsequent cases.

Although there appears to be little authority on the point, it is generally accepted by conveyancers that partnerships cannot hold the title to heritable property (at least in so far as it is held on feudal tenure) in the name of the partnership. To avoid this difficulty the title to heritable property is frequently taken in the name of one or more partners as trustees for the partnership. This problem will disappear upon the abolition of the feudal system as all property may then be held in the name of the partnership (see Scottish Law Commission, *Report on the Abolition of the Feudal System*, No. 168, para. 9.28 and draft Bill, clause 64).

In terms of the Conveyancing and Feudal Reform (Scotland) Act 1970, s. 27(1) a creditor in a standard security who sells the security subjects holds the sale proceeds in trust to be applied to specified purposes. The last of these purposes is payment of the residue (if any) to the debtor.

Where a group of tenants in a number of leases held of the same landlord wish to purchase the interest of their landlord but do not wish the leasehold relationship to be extinguished, the title to the landlord's interest is frequently taken in the name of a trust. The purposes of the trust are usually stated to be generally for the benefit of the tenants and the local community. This situation is sometimes encountered in relation to the purchase of highland estates where the existing tenants are crofters who wish to have more control over their affairs but do not wish to lose the security of tenure under the crofting legislation and other benefits which effeir to them as tenants. It may be impossible for the relationship of landlord and tenant to continue if a trust established by a single tenant with only that tenant as a beneficiary purchases the landlord's interest (*cf. Kildrummy (Jersey) Ltd v. IRC* (1992) where it was held that a lease granted by a party to a trustee holding only for the granter of the lease as sole beneficiary is a nullity).

3. CLASSIFICATION OF TRUSTS

TYPES OF TRUSTS

Trusts may be classified into various types as follows:

(a) discretionary trusts;
(b) simple and special trusts;
(c) *inter vivos* and testamentary trusts;
(d) public and private trusts;
(e) charitable trusts and other trusts; and
(f) trusts created voluntarily and those created by legal implication.

A trust may fall into a number of these categories. For example, one trust may be an *inter vivos* discretionary private trust. Another trust may be a testamentary charitable public trust.

Discretionary trusts
In Scots law there is no special category of trusts known as "discretionary trusts" to which different legal rules apply.

The word "discretion", however, is of considerable importance in relation to virtually all trusts because the trustees will require to exercise some element of discretion. For example, from time to time trustees may require to decide to retain or sell certain investments. In this sense, the exercise of discretion is more properly classified as a duty rather than a power of the trustees.

The discretion afforded to trustees in a trust deed can make a trust a very flexible device. In relation to both public and private trusts the discretion may be administrative or dispositive. The trustees may be given discretion in relation to administrative matters such as the timing of the sale of investments or matters relating to the day-to-day administration of the trust. In other cases the discretion may extend to matters such as who is to benefit from the trust, the size or nature of their shares and the timing of the vesting of the benefits.

Simple and special trusts
In a special trust the trust property is held for a special purpose. With a special trust, the purposes of the trust are set out, and the trustee has duties to perform in accordance with the truster's directions. An example is when a truster directs his trustees to hold property for A in liferent and for B in fee.

In a simple trust there is no special trust purpose but merely an obligation to hold the property and to hand it over to the truster or his nominee when called upon to do so. Thus, a simple trust arises when property is held by the individual partners of a firm for behoof of the firm.

Inter vivos and testamentary trusts
Inter vivos trusts are set up by trusters whilst they are alive. Testamentary or *mortis causa* trusts are set up to take effect after the death of the truster.

A good example of a testamentary trustee is an executor appointed under a will who administers the estate of the deceased for the purposes of distribution amongst the beneficiaries.

Public and private trusts

Private trusts are for the benefit of individuals and cannot continue indefinitely. Public trusts are for the benefit of the public or a section of the public and can exist indefinitely.

It may sometimes be difficult to determine whether a trust is a public trust or a private trust because of the problem of distinguishing between a large group of individuals and a small section of the general public. This is illustrated in *Salvesen's Trs v. Wye* (1954) where a testator left a legacy to his "poor relatives, friends or acquaintances". As this could potentially have been a very wide class the question was how to determine whether this was a private or public trust? Lord President Cooper held that the "dominant determining factor" which defined the potential beneficiaries was the fact of their connection with the testator and not the fact of their poverty. Applying this test, he held that the wording employed established a private trust rather than a public trust. Not all cases are capable of such clear distinction and a particularly difficult case is *Glentanar v. Scottish Industrial Musical Association* (1925). In this case the truster donated a silver shield to a musical association for the purpose of having the shield awarded as a trophy to the winner of an annual musical feis organised by the trustees. It was held that this was a private trust and not a public trust but the decision is not free from criticism because there are strong indications of public benefit in the gift.

In relation to private trusts, all identifiable beneficiaries and the truster have title to sue the trustees in cases of failure to carry out trust purposes. Obviously in the case of *mortis causa* trustees the truster will not be in a position to raise legal proceedings. Because public trusts are for the benefit of at least a section of the public, any member of that section of the public who would qualify as a potential beneficiary and, in addition, the Lord Advocate representing the public interest, can bring an action to enforce the provisions of the trust. There is some legal debate as to whether this form of action is truly an action known as an *actio popularis* which is employed to enforce other public rights such as public rights of way or certain regalian rights such as the right to recreate on the foreshore. Nevertheless, in many trust cases the class of parties who truly have a right to enforce a public trust will be so broad as to render the action one which is an *actio popularis* or at very least an action which resembles an *actio popularis* in almost all respects. An example is to be seen in *Ross v. George Heriot's Hospital* (1843). In that case the founder of George Heriot's Hospital declared in his will that the school would admit poor fatherless children who were sons of the freemen and burgesses of Edinburgh. A certain boy was qualified as his father, who was a freeman and burgess, was dead. He applied to the school and was refused entry by the governors. He brought an action to gain entry and it was held that he was entitled to bring such an action. The form of the action was an *actio popularis*.

In private trusts the truster has the right to appoint new trustees in a situation where the old trustees fail, such as on the death of the last trustee. This is the case even if such a right is not expressly reserved in the trust deed. (For an example of the existence of this power see *Glentanar v. Scottish Industrial Musical Association* (1925).) Such a power does not exist in relation to public trusts except where the truster has reserved this right by special stipulation in the trust deed. It will not exist in cases of silence.

The courts can exercise a wider jurisdiction over the administration of public trusts than they can over private trusts. The most notable instance of this in relation to public trusts is the exercise of the *nobile officium* of the court to sanction a *cy-près* scheme (see pp. 78–82). Such oversight is not available in relation to private trusts which have different rules for variation (see pp. 75–78).

It is probable that in questions of the construction of trust deeds the courts are more liberal in their approach to the words used where the trust is a public trust. Broadly speaking, this has the effect that the courts will make a greater effort to save the validity of a public trust than a private trust. This may be exemplified in cases relative to public trusts where the courts have sustained the trust for purposes as vaguely stated as a trust for "charities" (see, further p. 28).

Charitable trusts
In English law there is an important class of trusts known as "charitable" trusts which are distinct from "private" trusts. Although many trusts are set up in Scotland to further charitable purposes, this classification as "charitable trusts" does not generally exist in Scots law except in relation to taxation law.

When construing a United Kingdom taxation statute the word "charity" and "charitable" must be given the technical meaning given to them in English law. For authority, see *Inland Revenue v. Glasgow Police Athletic Association* (1953). To qualify as a charitable trust for tax purposes, a trust must be for the relief of poverty, the advancement of religion, the advancement of education or for "other purposes beneficial to the community".

Certain of these "charitable" trusts may become what is known as a "recognised body" in terms of the Law Reform (Miscellaneous Provisions) (Scotland) Act 1990, Pt I. If they are such a recognised body they are entitled to describe themselves as a "Scottish charity". There is considerable regulation of the affairs of these bodies in terms of the 1990 Act (see pp. 72–74).

Creation by voluntary act or legal implication
The constitution or creation of trusts varies according to the nature of the trust.

Where a truster grants a trust deed either *inter vivos* or *mortis causa* that is an instance of a trust created voluntarily. In such a situation the truster intends to transfer his property to trustees for the achievement of certain purposes chosen by him. For example, in the context of a breach of trust by a trustee who receives profits from trust business as a result of a conflict of interest, a constructive trust arises on receipt of the profits. No deed of trust is needed.

Where a trust is created by legal implication the trust arises independently of the wishes of the parties involved. The law merely imposes a trust on the parties because of the factual circumstances in which they find themselves. The aim of the law in such situations is usually to provide proprietorial remedies in the absence of express provision.

Voluntarily created trusts

A trust may be created by the express will of a truster as set out in a document of trust. An express trust may be constituted in three different types of deed, as follows:

(a) a disposition to the trustee bearing to be in trust only;
(b) a disposition to the trustee which is *ex facie* absolute but qualified by a separate declaration or acknowledgement of the trust purposes; and
(c) a declaration of trust by a person who is already vested in the property.

What all three methods of creation have in common is the passing of property from the truster to the trustee for certain purposes. In all cases the intention to create a trust should be expressed clearly otherwise problems of interpretation may arise. To rescue the situation the court may have to resort to the notion of the precatory trust (see below).

A trust is in essence a proprietorial relationship and the title of the trustees to the property to be subject to the trust is not complete until delivery of that property to the trustees. In relation to heritable property, actual delivery is impossible and when property is transferred to a trust the recording of that deed in the Sasine register or the registration of the disposition in the Land Register of Scotland is regarded as the equivalent of delivery (see p. 85).

Where the truster and the trustee are the same person there can be no actual delivery of the property. Instead, there must be some delivery or equivalent of delivery such as intimation of the trust to third parties which operates as an irrevocable divestiture of the truster and investiture in himself as trustee. This question has given rise to considerable discussion in matters of taxation and constitution of securities over moveables. The general rule appears to be that intimation to third parties must take place after the creation of the trust. Intimation before creation of the trust is not sufficient.

Considerable debate about the issue of delivery of property in the context of a trust has arisen in connection with what are known as "retention of title" clauses or "Romalpa" clauses and the limits of the concept are still not well defined in the relevant case law (see, *e.g. Clark Taylor & Co. Ltd v. Quality Site Development (Edinburgh) Ltd* (1981)).

A testamentary trust is set up by the death of the truster which makes the trust irrevocable. Otherwise stated, in *mortis causa* trusts, death is regarded as the equivalent of delivery.

Trusts implied from unclear words — precatory trusts

Precatory trusts may arise where a person conveys estate to a donee but uses unclear or loose wording and there is some uncertainty as to whether he intended to create a trust. Strictly speaking, the courts construe the words employed by the person to decide whether he wanted to create a trust. Realistically such a view is slightly artificial. What the courts are really doing is determining the wishes of the party and deciding whether a trust is the method of giving effect to them. In theory, however, the trust arises from the words used by the testator: hence such a trust is one which may be said to be voluntarily created by a truster rather than a trust implied by law.

The main type of question which arises is whether the party's directions in respect of the estate should be construed as imperative or whether they amount to a mere wish or request. If they are the latter, no trust is created, but if his words are construed as intending to impose on the donee an obligation to deal with the estate in the manner specified, a trust may be held to be constituted by the "precatory" words. The test is whether the deed can fairly be read as imposing an obligation on the donee to deal with the estate in the way specified by the donor. If it does the courts will declare that a trust has been created.

This situation crops up most frequently in relation to informally drawn-up wills. A distinction is drawn between wishes directed to an executor and those to a beneficiary. The former are more likely to constitute a trust and this is illustrated in a number of contrasting cases. On the one hand it has been held that where a truster "preferred" that his trustees pay a capital sum to a legatee this was held to constitute a trust (*Reid's Trs v. Dawson* (1915)), as was the case where a testator "authorised" his widow to dispose of his estate in accordance with his instructions (*Reddie's Trs v. Lindsay* (1890)). On the other hand, where a testatrix stated that she "would like" her husband to give part of her estate to certain named persons, it was held that no trust obligation was created (*Wilson v. Lindsay* (1879)). Likewise, where it was the testator's "anxious desire" and "hope" that his wife should bequeath a half share of what she had at her death to certain relations, this gave them no enforceable claim when she died without carrying out her husband's wishes (*Barclay's Exr v. McLeod* (1880)).

FORMAL VALIDITY OF TRUST DEEDS

The relevant legislation is contained in the Requirements of Writing (Scotland) Act 1995. The Act is also relevant in relation to execution of wills and testamentary deeds but in the context of trusts the most important points are as follows:

(1) The general rule is that writing is not required for the constitution of a trust (1995 Act, s. 1(1)). This is subject to three exceptions:
  (a) Where a person declares himself to be sole trustee of his own property or any property which he may acquire (1995 Act, s. 1(2)(a)(iii)).
  (b) Any trust which relates to an interest in land will require to be in writing (1995 Act, s. 1(2)(b)). The term "interest in land" is not defined in the 1995 Act but it is generally considered that it includes all the known real rights relating to land and property such as rights of ownership, leases (enduring over one year), servitudes, liferents and heritable securities. *Inter vivos* trusts which relate to moveables do not need to be in writing.

    (c) Writing is always required for any trust created by a will or
testamentary disposition (1995 Act, s. 1(2)(c)). Writing is not required
for *inter vivos* trusts unless they fall within the two previous
exceptions.
(2) Despite the provisions of the statute it is prudent to ensure, where a
client wishes to set up a trust, that all the provisions relative to that trust
are put into writing.
(3) The 1995 Act contains further provisions about subscription and the
self-proving status of the subscription of documents generally. These
rules will not be examined here but it is clear that a deed of trust is a
document and that these rules will apply where appropriate.

LEGALLY-IMPLIED TRUSTS

The law will imply that a trust is created in certain specific circumstances.
There are various types of trusts created by legal implication and they may
be sub-classified into four different types:

(1) constructive trusts;
(2) resulting trusts;
(3) fiduciary fees; and
(4) trusts created by statute.

These will be examined in the following paragraphs.

Constructive trusts

In England constructive trusts are recognised in many situations but Scottish
authority (*e.g. Black v. Brown* (1982)) recognises only two situations in
which constructive trusts may arise.

    The first situation is where a person holding a fiduciary position obtains
some personal benefit from that position. He is then deemed to be holding
the benefit as trustee for the beneficiaries. The classic example of this is
where a trustee makes a profit from carrying on the truster's business.
On the principle that a trustee should not act as *auctor in rem suam* (see pp. 52–59)
the trustee is deemed to hold such a benefit or profit for the benefit of the
beneficiaries under the original trust (see *Cherry's Trs v. Patrick* (1911)). In
this case a trustee in a testamentary trust continued to supply goods to the
business of the truster being carried on by the trustees after the death of
the truster. He made no extra profit and was simply doing what he had been
doing before the death of the testator. It was held that the trustee was under
a constructive trust to pay back to the trust all profit from this series of sales
of goods.

    The second situation is where a third party, either gratuitously (meaning
for no valuable consideration) or with knowledge of the breach of trust,
acquires property belonging to a trust. In such a case he is regarded as
holding the property as trustee for the beneficiaries (see *Soar v. Ashwell*
(1893)).

Resulting Trusts

A resulting trust is where the property "results" or falls back into the beneficial ownership of the truster (or his representatives) by virtue of his radical or reversionary right. For example, when the trust purposes fail, the property is held by the trustees for the benefit of the truster (or his representatives). Resulting trusts are a device implied by law to deal with the situation where the beneficial interest in the trust estate is not effectually disposed of and cannot be assigned elsewhere.

Resulting trusts cannot arise where it is clear that the truster excludes their operation either by express statement or sufficient implication, as would be the case where he indicates that he has divested himself of all interest in the trust property.

Resulting trusts cannot arise if the trust is one to which the *cy-près* jurisdiction can be applied or if an application can be made for rearrangement of the trust under the Law Reform (Miscellaneous Provisions) (Scotland) Act 1990, s. 9.

Resulting trusts have been held to arise where the trust purposes are contrary to public policy or impossible to carry out (see *McCaig's Trustees v. Kirk Session of the United Free Church of Lismore* (1915)).

Similarly, a resulting trust arises where the truster has failed to appoint trustees (*Angus's Exx v. Batchan's Trs* (1949)) or where trust purposes fail from uncertainty (*Anderson v. Smoke* (1898)). In this case daughters were directed to hold certain money in trust for behoof of their brother. If the trust money was not disposed of during the brother's lifetime, it was provided that it was to be disposed of in any way they should think proper. It was held that the phrase "in any way they should think proper" was void from uncertainty, and consequently a resulting trust was deemed to have arisen in favour of the residuary beneficiary of the truster's testamentary settlement.

A resulting trust will not arise where there is merely a temporary uncertainty as to what are the trust purposes or a postponement of their coming into operation. For example, in *Templeton v. Burgh of Ayr* (1910) funds were placed in trust for the purpose of the rebuilding of a ⊦ridge. The bridge was actually repaired from other funds and it was held that no resulting trust arose as the trust funds might be used at some time in the future for further repairs and maintenance.

Fiduciary fees

This occurs where property is granted in liferent to A and in fee to persons unborn or incapable of ascertainment.

In this context the law has to prevent the fee being *in pendente* (which might loosely be translated as being in "hyperspace" or owned by nobody) which is generally regarded as a legal impossibility. (There is no such thing in Scotland as ownerless property — Scots law will always try to find an owner of property). Where property is granted in liferent to A and in fee to persons unborn or incapable of ascertainment the party A is treated as a fiduciary fiar. He holds the fee in trust for the ultimate beneficiaries and he may be granted, by the court, all the powers of a trustee at common law or under the Trusts (Scotland) Act 1921.

When the beneficial fiar (the unborn child) is ascertained the fiduciary fee comes to an end (*Snell v. White* (1872)).

If the unborn child never does come into existence the fiduciary fiar does not keep the estate. Instead, the estate reverts back to the granter.

The trustee's powers of administration in this peculiar trust are limited when compared to the powers of a trustee in a normal trust. In terms of the Trusts (Scotland) Act 1921, s. 8(2) the fiduciary fiar does not have the usual powers of a trustee. Instead he must apply to the court either for authority to exercise any power competent to a trustee, or for the appointment of an independent trustee who will act on behalf of both liferenter and fiar.

A fiduciary fiar is subject to the normal obligations of a trustee, including the duty not to be *auctor in rem suam*.

Trusts created by statute

There are numerous examples of these. Only three examples which are commonly encountered in practice will be noted here.

One notable example is a trust of a policy of assurance effected by a married man on his own life and expressed on the face of it to be for the benefit of his wife or children or both. This is deemed to be a trust for them (Married Women's Policies of Assurance (Scotland) Act 1880, s. 2). This has now been amended to apply to a trust of a policy of assurance effected by a married woman in the same way (Married Women's Policies of Assurance (Scotland) (Amendment) Act 1980, s. 1). These policies are commonly used in connection with house purchases.

In terms of the Conveyancing and Feudal Reform (Scotland) Act 1970, s. 27(1) a creditor in a standard security who sells the security subjects holds the sale proceeds in trust to be applied to specified purposes. The last of these purposes is payment of the residue (if any) to the debtor.

In terms of the Companies Act 1985, ss. 313(2) and 316(1) provision is made for sums received by a director in breach of certain statutory prohibitions relating to unlawful payments for loss of office or as consideration for or in connection with his retirement from office to be held in trust. This may occur in two situations: (a) where undisclosed and unapproved payment is made in connection with the transfer of the whole or any part of the undertaking of the company and (b) where undisclosed and unapproved payment is made in connection with certain offers for shares. Where such unlawful payments are made to the director the sums are deemed to be held in trust by the director for the company (s. 313) or for the persons who have sold their shares as a result of the offer made (s. 316).

---

4. PARTIES AND PROPERTY

WHO MAY BE A TRUSTER?

As a general rule anyone who can competently alienate property in his possession can create a trust. This usually means persons of full age and capacity.

Persons of unsound mind cannot create a trust. Not all types of mental illness will be sufficient to bring this rule into operation. Only if the mentally ill person lacks the understanding of what he is doing will this render his attempt to create a trust invalid.

Certain limitations arise out of the terms of the Age of Legal Capacity (Scotland) Act 1991. In terms of the 1991 Act, s. 1(1)(a) persons under 16 cannot create any form of trust. In terms of the 1991 Act, s. 2(2) a person over 12 has testamentary capacity and so can create a testamentary trust. In terms of the 1985 Act, s. 2(1) a person under 16 has no capacity to create an *inter vivos* trust. A person of or over the age of 16 can create such a trust but if he was under the age of 18 at the date of the transaction he can, until he attains the age of 21, apply to the court to have the transaction set aside as a prejudicial transaction. It will be considered a prejudicial transaction if it is a transaction which an adult, exercising reasonable prudence, would not have entered into in the circumstances of the applicant at the time of entering into the transaction (1991 Act, s. 3).

Under earlier law certain parties were subjected to disabilities and were unable to create trusts. Such parties, who are now subject to no disabilities include: married women, aliens, bastards (illegitimate children) or criminals.

The Crown can convey property into a trust (see Crown Private Estates Act 1862, s. 6).

WHO MAY BE A TRUSTEE?

Generally speaking any person who has the legal capacity to hold and deal with property is qualified to act as a trustee. It has been said that the creator of a trust "can select as his trustee any person he chooses of whatever character" — *per* Chitty J. in *Tempest v. Camoys* (1888). This means that in a trust deed a truster may exclude certain persons from acting as his trustee. It is in his discretion to do so. For example, in a trust deed the truster may declare that only persons who support a particular football club may be trustees under a trust set up by him.

Subject to any such express provision in the trust deed, the matter is dealt with by the common law which is subject to special statutory provision in particular cases.

An insane person cannot accept office as a trustee. The issue of insanity more often arises as a ground for removal of a trustee from office. The reason for this is that even if the trustee is actually insane at the time of his appointment this insanity will not have been judicially determined at that time. It should be noted that all forms of mental illness do not amount to insanity. Only if the insanity is sufficiently severe to prevent an understanding of the powers, duties and responsibilities of the office of trusteeship will this be sufficient to exclude a party from being a trustee. Mild forms of mental illness and mere eccentricity are not enough to disqualify a person.

A person under 16 cannot be a trustee (Age of Legal Capacity (Scotland) Act 1991, ss. 1(1) and 9(5)).

An insolvent party (even if he has been sequestrated) is not generally disqualified from being a trustee. There are a number of special rules which disqualify a bankrupt party from being a particular type of trustee. For example, bankruptcy renders an individual ineligible for appointment as a judicial factor. In charitable trusts there are special rules to disqualify insolvent parties (Law Reform (Miscellaneous Provisions) (Scotland) Act 1990, s. 8).

A party convicted of a crime, other than high treason, is not generally disqualified from being a trustee. In charitable trusts there are special rules to disqualify those convicted of crimes involving dishonesty (Law Reform (Miscellaneous Provisions) (Scotland) Act 1990, s. 8). If the convicted party is incarcerated and as a prisoner is incapable of performing his duties as a trustee to the extent that this would prejudice the administration of the trust, the appointment of such a party as a trustee may be void. In practice, criminal guilt seems more likely to be founded upon as a ground for removal of a trustee than as a disqualification for the office.

In relation to *mortis causa* trusts, a party who has killed the testator may not be appointed as the executor of the deceased (*Smith, Ptr* (1979)). The provisions of the Forfeiture Act 1982 are limited to modifications from disqualification in respect of a "beneficial interest" in certain interests in property and appear to be insufficiently broad to permit appointment as executor (see 1982 Act, s. 2(4)).

An alien is not disqualified from being a trustee unless he is an enemy alien. Statutory provisions (British Nationality and Status of Aliens Act 1914, s. 17, as amended by British Nationality Act 1948, Sched. 4, Pt 2) have revoked the common law rule whereby an alien could not have a right or title to heritable property in Scotland but it remains the law that an alien cannot be the owner of a British ship either beneficially or in trust. It is also not permissible for aircraft to be registered in the United Kingdom in the name of an alien (Air Navigation Order 1989 (S.I. 1989 No. 2004, as amended by subsequent regulations).

Residence abroad is no bar to trusteeship, although by statute it is made a ground on which, in certain circumstances, the court may remove a trustee (1921 Act, s. 23). Nevertheless the terms of a trust may include conditions as to residence. With modern facilities for travel and communication such residence must cause less inconvenience than in former times. Again this general statement is subject to particular exceptions. For example, in the context of sequestration, only persons who reside within the jurisdiction of the Court of Session may be appointed permanent trustee (Bankruptcy (Scotland) Act 1984, s. 24(2)(d)).

The Crown in its public capacity may act as a trustee and in such capacity it is a corporation which never dies. Mrs Elizabeth Windsor may also act as a trustee as a private individual but, in such a private capacity, she is a mortal individual. The Crown in its public capacity acts as trustee for the public in relation to certain rights and properties which are known as regalian rights (otherwise known as rights which fall *inter regalia*). Examples of these are the public right to recreate on the foreshore and to white fishing in the territorial sea and, possibly also, public rights of way. The Crown retains a title to enforce these rights on behalf of the general public in addition to the separate right of each member of the general public to enforce the rights by *actio popularis*.

A foreign government may be a trustee provided that it is not an enemy government.

As a general rule, public bodies such as local authorities may be trustees. This is exemplified in *Martin v. City of Edinburgh District Council* (1988).

Companies incorporated under the companies legislation may be trustees but there are certain special factors which are examined below.

LIMITED COMPANIES AS TRUSTEES

Firms of solicitors or banks often incorporate special limited liability companies to act as executors or as trustees. The reason for this is to make sure that the firms or banks are not responsible for the extensive liabilities of a trustee should matters go wrong. An example of an occasion where a trustee company was not used, but instead the estate was administered by the in-house trustee department of a bank is seen in *Grant v. Grant's Exrs* (1994). In this case the executors were the Royal Bank of Scotland and the bank was held liable for payment of incorrect beneficiaries.

Where limited companies are incorporated for the purpose of being a trustee or executor it is likely that they will have specialised provisions in the objects clause of their Memorandum of Association.

One benefit of a corporate trustee is that it never dies and thus avoids the difficulties in relation to continuity of administration which arise where a natural person dies and that person is a sole trustee. In *Leith's Exr* (1937) this benefit was a factor in the appointment of a new trustee by the court under the Trusts (Scotland) Act 1921, s. 22.

The courts have expressed some dislike of such trust companies. For example, in *Ommanney, Ptr* (1966) the court refused a variation under the Trusts (Scotland) Act 1961, s.1 insofar as it involved a bank being appointed trustee. The reason given by the court was that such a corporate body was not a suitable party to exercise discretion involving personal and family considerations.

In connection with special trustees there are some exceptions to the general rule that companies incorporated under the companies legislation may be trustees. For example, a limited company or partnership or any other non-natural person cannot be appointed as a judicial factor largely because individual responsibility to the court is an essential feature of the office. Similarly, in the context of the law of bankruptcy only individuals and not corporations or firms may be permanent trustees on the estate of the sequestrated party.

Under certain statutes the purpose of the trust favours statutory trustees. For example in relation to unit trusts there is a requirement that a corporate trustee with substantial capital reserves is appointed (Financial Services Act 1986, s. 78).

EX OFFICIO TRUSTEES

Most trustees are appointed as individuals and the trust deed or other deed of appointment expressly names them as individuals. In certain other cases the holder of an office from time to time is appointed as a trustee.

A good example of this matter occurs in relation to clubs. In such cases the office-bearers from time to time (such as the president, vice-president, treasurer and secretary) are nominated as trustees. Other common examples of this nature include churches where the trustees may be the deacons of the church or a group of other office-bearers such as bishops.

In a case such as a club a person becomes a trustee upon the acceptance of the office within the club. If the person accepts the office within the club he cannot refuse to be a trustee. When that person ceases to be the relevant office-bearer he ceases to be the trustee. Matters are different where the trust nominates the office-holder in an outside organisation to be the trustee. For example, a trust deed providing for the relief of the poor may nominate as trustees certain office-bearers in the local authority. In such a case, a person accepting the office in the outside body may refuse to become a trustee because it is not a condition of his appointment to his post as office-bearer (see, *Mags of Edinburgh v. McLaren* (1881)).

There are special statutory rules for the transfer of titles to land held by *ex officio* trustees and these rules avoid the need for detailed conveyancing upon the appointment of new office bearers (see Conveyancing (Scotland) Act 1874 and Titles to Land Consolidation (Scotland) Act 1868, s. 26).

WHO MAY BE A BENEFICIARY?

Generally speaking it is the truster who identifies who the beneficiaries are under the trust which he sets up. He may limit the class of persons who may be beneficiaries and such limitations will be applied. Subject to such express limitations the common law will govern the position as follows:

(1) Any person, legal or natural, may be a beneficiary. So a limited company, a firm (partnership), a university, a hospital trust or a corporation may be a beneficiary.

(2) A beneficiary may be insane, not yet born or belong to a prescribed class of unascertained persons.

(3) A witness to the trust deed may be a beneficiary but it is more prudent to ensure that all witnesses are independent to avoid the deed being challenged on the basis of doctrines such as undue influence or facility and circumvention.

(4) In a strict sense animals cannot be the beneficiaries of a trust because they lack legal personality. This, however, does not prevent the creation of trusts for the maintenance of animals. Frequently a testator will make provision in his will for the care of a pet after his death and such a provision will be regarded as valid. Other aspects of such a trust are examined above.

(5) In relation to provisions in *mortis causa* trusts a party who has killed the testator may not take a benefit under the trust. This is known as the rule of the "unworthy heir" and is founded in both common law and statute (*Smith, Ptr* (1979); Parricide Act 1594). Modification but not complete relief from disqualification may be sought under the Forfeiture Act 1982 (see *Cross, Ptr* (1987)).

WHAT PROPERTY MAY BE SUBJECT TO A TRUST?

Subject to a number of qualifications outlined below, any property which can be alienated may be the subject of a trust. This includes heritage, moveables, corporeal property and incorporeal property.

A right to a peerage cannot be the subject of a trust (see *The Buckhurst Peerage* (1876)). The reason for this is that such a title is attached to a person and cannot be separated from that person. You should note that a barony title is not a peerage and land which is held on a barony title may be subject to a trust.

A trust of foreign land is invalid if the legal system where the land is situated does not give effect to trusts (*Brown's Trs v. Gregson* (1920)). In that case a testator who was domiciled in Scotland conveyed his whole estate (including immoveable property in Argentina) to trustees in trust for children. By Argentinean law, trusts were not recognised or given effect. The settlement was declared null as regards the Argentinean property by the Argentinean courts and this Argentinean decision was recognised by Scots law.

A trust deed may make specific provision that a particular trust should not include a particular type of property in its assets. For example, even although as a general rule heritable property throughout Scotland may be owned by a trust, the truster may expressly state that trustees should avoid purchasing heritable property in a particular place.

Although investments, such as shares in limited companies, may be owned by trusts there are some statutory limitations on the amount of such investments which may be owned by trusts at any one time. These limitations are largely contained in the Trustee Investments Act 1961 and will be examined in relation to trustees' power to invest (see pp. 44–52).

WHO OWNS TRUST PROPERTY? — THE TRUSTEES

The real right of property in trust property rests with the trustees. They are the owners of trust property (*per* Lord Moncrieff in *Inland Revenue v. Clark's Trs* (1939)). Nevertheless the trustees' right to the property is constrained by the right of the beneficiaries and they cannot use the trust property for their own purposes as if it were their own property.

The trust property is not available for the satisfaction of the trustees' personal debts (*Heritable Reversionary Co. Ltd v. Millar* (1891)). Upon the sequestration of a debtor any property held by him in trust for any other person does not vest in the permanent trustee (Bankruptcy (Scotland) Act 1985, s. 33(1)(b)).

In the context of heritable property it is the names of the trustees which are on the title deeds. When property is purchased or sold by a trust the missives of sale and purchase are entered into by or on behalf of the trustees and not by or on behalf of the beneficiaries.

Where there is more than one trustee the type of ownership is joint ownership (as opposed to common ownership). On the death or resignation of one trustee the share of the deceased or resigning trustee accresses to the remaining trustees without the necessity of any conveyance.

Each trustee cannot separately dispose of his own share or burden it with a security.

The property is not that of the trustee as an individual and such property cannot be affected by the diligence of a trustee's personal creditors. Because a party who is a trustee acts in a different capacity as a trustee and as an individual, he may enter into a contract with one party being himself as an individual and the other with himself as a trustee although such an arrangement may be voidable under conflict of interest rules. Similarly he may acquire a real right such as a servitude to be enjoyed by himself as an individual over land owned by himself as trustee.

THE RIGHT OF THE BENEFICIARIES TO TRUST PROPERTY

The beneficiaries and the truster have independent personal rights to require the trustees to carry out the trust purposes but they are not the owners and they do not have real rights in the trust property.

Although the right of the beneficiaries may be classified as a personal right, it has certain special attributes which gives it greater strength than other personal rights such as contractual rights. So strong is the beneficiaries' right that some commentators view it as "anomalous in nature" and state that it can be categorised neither as a purely personal right nor as a real right of property. This categorisation has some merit, but it does not clarify matters a great deal. In some respects the beneficiaries' right is like a real right in that the beneficiaries' right is preferred to the claims of a trustee's personal creditors in the event of a sequestration. Also, the beneficiaries right is not defeated by the alienation of trust property in breach of trust, as long as the person acquiring it either has not given full value for the property or has acquired it with actual or constructive knowledge of the trust. Nevertheless the beneficiaries' right does not go as far as a real right because one category of acquirer in breach of trust can defeat their right, namely the *bona fide* onerous transferee without notice of the trust. It is obvious that the Scots law of trusts requires much clearer theoretical analysis in relation to these matters.

The interest of the beneficiary can be transferred to a third party by assignation. If an alimentary liferent is assigned the court will fix a reasonable alimentary allowance so that any excess can be paid by the trustees to the assignee (*Craig v. Pearson's Trs* (1915)). To complete the assignee's right, the assignation must be intimated to the trustees. If this is not done the trustee in the beneficiary's sequestration will be preferred to the assignee (*Tod's Trs v. Wilson* (1869)).

---

5. APPOINTMENT, ASSUMPTION AND RESIGNATION OF TRUSTEES

APPOINTMENT OF ORIGINAL TRUSTEES BY TRUSTER

It is generally the case that a party setting up a trust nominates the parties he wishes to be trustees in the deed of trust. These are the "original trustees".

These parties must have capacity to be trustees and the appointment is not valid until there is an acceptance by the parties nominated.

There is no form of nomination or acceptance prescribed by the common law or statute but in each case it is best if the matter is dealt with in a clearly expressed deed. Ambiguity and difficulty may arise where a person makes no formal acceptance of the office of trusteeship but acts as if he were the trustee. In *Ker v. City of Glasgow Bank* (1879) a man who had never formally accepted the office of trusteeship permitted his name to be used as a trustee in a stock transfer and signed this with the word "trustee" appearing after his name. It was held that he had impliedly accepted the office of trustee.

As a general rule, acceptance is a voluntary act and no one is obliged to accept trusteeship. There are two exceptions to this:

(a) Where the trustee in question is an *ex officio* trustee — such as occurs frequently in relation to the officers of clubs, churches or other voluntary associations — acceptance of the office within the club or church means that the individual becomes the trustee. Provided the office is within the club, he cannot accept the office and refuse to be a trustee. Matters are different where the office is outwith the club (see pp. 19–20).

(b) Where a person becomes a trustee by operation of law, such as would be the case in a resulting trust or a constructive trust, the wishes of that person are irrelevant.

APPOINTMENT OF CERTAIN SPECIAL TRUSTEES

Executors may be appointed either by the deceased or the court. An executor appointed by the deceased is known as an executor nominate. An executor appointed by the court is an executor dative.

To complete his title to the estate of the deceased an executor must obtain confirmation from the court. To obtain such confirmation the executor must exhibit a full and true inventory of all the estate of the deceased already recovered or known to be existing. Confirmation cannot be granted to any estate not in the inventory.

If there is no person who can be confirmed as executor nominate or if the executor nominate takes no steps to expede (obtain) confirmation it is necessary to apply to the court for appointment as an executor dative. A person cannot be appointed as executor dative on the grounds of expediency; instead the person appointed must have a legal title to the office. Interest in the succession (in other words entitlement to succeed under the will or on intestacy) is the general ground of confirmation. There is a detailed order of persons who are so entitled, which will not be dealt with here. (See Wilson and Duncan, *Trusts, Trustees and Executors* (2nd ed.), paras 32–49 to 32–61).

In terms of the Bankruptcy (Scotland) Act 1985, ss. 24 and 25 the permanent trustee is declared by the sheriff after election by the creditors and has an act and warrant issued to him by the sheriff clerk.

ASSUMPTION OF NEW TRUSTEES BY EXISTING TRUSTEES

New trustees may be assumed by existing trustees unless this power is expressly excluded by the trust deed, which is most unlikely (Trusts (Scotland) Act 1921, s. 3(b)). In some cases where the truster reserves to himself the power to appoint new trustees this will impliedly exclude the power of the trustees to assume new trustees (see *Munro's Trs v. Young* (1887)).

In relation to public trusts which have charitable status for revenue purposes the existing trustees have power to assume such new trustees as will bring the number up to three even if this is expressly excluded in the trust deed (Law Reform (Miscellaneous Provisions) (Scotland) Act 1990, s. 13).

In *Winning & Ors, Ptrs* (1999) it was confirmed that *ex-officio* trustees may assume new *ex-officio* trustees in exercise of the implied power to assume new trustees conferred in the Trusts (Scotland) Act 1921, s. 3(b).

The same considerations about acceptance of office exist in relation to new trustees as they do in respect of the original trustees. If the trust deed limits the parties who may be trustees to a class of persons, new trustees must also be selected from that class.

APPOINTMENT OF NEW TRUSTEES BY TRUSTER

In rare circumstances a provision in the trust deed may reserve to the truster the power to appoint new trustees in such circumstances as the trust deed specifies.

In the absence of any such provision the truster has no power to appoint new trustees. One exceptional case is private trusts, where the truster can appoint new trustees if the original trustees have failed and the exercise of the power is necessary to prevent the trust lapsing. The power does not exist in relation to public trusts.

APPOINTMENT OF NEW TRUSTEES BY THIRD PARTIES

In rare circumstances a provision in the trust deed may grant to third parties — named strangers or the holders of certain offices: the power to appoint new trustees on the happening of such circumstances as the trust deed specifies.

There is special statutory provision for trusts which are charities to the effect that the Lord Advocate may appoint new trustees where the existing trustees are unwilling or unable to do so (Law Reform (Miscellaneous Provisions) (Scotland) Act 1990, s. 13).

APPOINTMENT OF NEW TRUSTEES BY THE COURT

New trustees may be appointed by the court in terms of common law and under statute. For almost all practical purposes the statutory power has replaced the common law power.

The common law power may still be used where the statute is inapplicable. Two examples are:

(a) to appoint a new trustee to remove deadlock amongst existing trustees. (*Aikman, Ptr* (1881)); and

(b) to appoint a new trustee when a sole trustee is removed for incompetence and the trust would otherwise have lapsed (*Lamont v. Lamont* (1908)).

The current statutory provision is the Trusts (Scotland) Act 1921, s. 22. This stipulates for the appointment of new trustees by the court when trustees cannot be assumed under any trust deed, or when the sole acting trustee has become *incapax* (incapable, for example, due to supervening insanity) or has been continuously absent from the United Kingdom or has otherwise disappeared for a period of six months. The court is either the Court of Session or the sheriff court.

Under the 1921 Act, s. 22 an application may be made by any party having an interest in the trust estate. This would include the truster, the beneficiaries and the trustees.

The typical case of the application of this statutory provision is where the trust has lapsed through the failure of the trustees by death or otherwise. It is also applicable where the inability to assume new trustees is the result of deadlock among the existing trustees.

DEATH OF A TRUSTEE

When a trustee dies he ceases to be a trustee. His executors do not automatically become trustee in his place.

Where one of several trustees dies his share in the title to the trust property accresses to the surviving trustees without necessity of any conveyance. The reason is that the title of trustees is a form of joint property and not common property.

Where the trustee who dies is a sole trustee different considerations apply. The title to the trust estate remains in the deceased sole trustee and has to be taken out of his name by a process of conveyancing. A statutory procedure is set out in the Trusts (Scotland) Act 1921, ss. 22 and 24. There is an alternative procedure which allows the executor of the last surviving trustee to add the trust property into the inventory attached to his confirmation and thus obtain judicial sanction to transfer the trust property to a person who may be legally authorised to continue the administration of the trust estate or, alternatively, direct to the beneficiaries if the administration is complete (see Executors (Scotland) Act 1900, s. 6 as amended by the Succession (Scotland) Act 1964, ss. 14(1), 34(1) and Sched. 2, para. 3).

If all of the executors are dead or are incapable of acting, confirmation *ad non executa* may be granted to any estate contained in the original confirmation which remains unuplifted or has not been transferred to the persons entitled thereto (Executors (Scotland) Act 1900, s. 7 as amended by the Succession (Scotland) Act 1964, Sched. 2, para. 14). Such confirmation may be granted to the person who would have been entitled to the original confirmation if the first executor had declined.

The death of certain special trustees is dealt with in particular statutes. For example, upon the death of a permanent trustee in a bankruptcy the creditors may elect a new permanent trustee who may be confirmed by the sheriff (Bankruptcy (Scotland) Act 1985, s. 28).

INSANITY OF TRUSTEE

Supervening insanity does not terminate the office of trusteeship; although it may be a ground for removal of the person from the office of trustee in terms of the Trusts (Scotland) Act 1921, s. 23 (see pp. 26–27).

The Trusts (Scotland) Act 1921, s. 23 also permits removal on the grounds of "incapacity... by reason of mental disability". This may permit removal of a trustee who suffers from psychiatric illness or weakness which falls short of insanity, provided it is sufficient materially to impair the trustee's ability to carry out his function.

Special statutory provision for such removal is made for particular types of trustees. For example, a permanent trustee who becomes insane may be removed from office under the Bankruptcy (Scotland) Act 1985, s. 29(9).

TRUSTEE'S POWER TO RESIGN

Gratuitous trustees other than sole trustees have a right to resign in terms of the Trusts (Scotland) Act 1921, s. 3(a) and proviso (1). The power to resign may only be excluded by express provision in the trust deed. The power will not be excluded by inference.

In terms of s. 3(a) and proviso (1) of the 1921 Act a sole trustee cannot resign his office unless he has assumed "new trustees" who have accepted office, or the court has appointed new trustees or a judicial factor. The section is badly worded and it is possible to argue that because the statute refers to "new trustees" (plural) a sole trustee must appoint more than one trustee before he can resign. In *Kennedy, Ptr* (1983) this argument was rejected and a sole executrix was permitted to resign when she appointed a single executor to act in her place. An exceptional case is made for a permanent trustee who may be permitted by the sheriff to resign even though a replacement has not been elected. It is more usual that election of a new permanent trustee will be made a condition of the permission to resign given by the sheriff to the permanent trustee (Bankruptcy (Scotland) Act 1985, s. 28(1A)).

A trustee appointed "on the footing" of receiving remuneration for his services cannot resign in the absence of an express power to do so (Trusts (Scotland) Act 1921, s. 3(a) and proviso (2)). The same applies to a trustee who has accepted a legacy, bequest or annuity on condition of accepting office as trustee, unless there is an express provision in the trust deed allowing him to resign.

Resignation is usually in express form but it may in rare circumstances, be implied from actings. Mere lapse of time does not amount to resignation.

A judicial factor cannot resign office without judicial authority (see Trusts (Scotland) Act 1921, s.3(a) and proviso (3)).

An executor nominate can resign: an executor dative cannot do so.

REMOVAL OF TRUSTEES

A trustee may be removed from office by the court for the limited reasons stated in the Trusts (Scotland) Act 1921, s. 23. This does not remove an existing common law power of the court to remove a trustee who persistently acts in a way which prejudices or obstructs the proper functioning of the trust. The grounds specified in the 1921 Act, s. 23 are:

(a) insanity;

(b) incapacity through mental or physical disability;

(c) continuous absence from the United Kingdom for at least six months; and

(d) disappearance for at least six months.

If the first or second ground is established the court must grant the application for removal. If the third and fourth grounds are established the court may grant the removal. The application may be made by a co-trustee, a beneficiary or other person interested in the trust estate. Where the trustee sought to be removed is a sole trustee, steps have to be taken to secure the continuance of the trust by the appointment of a judicial factor or by having the removed trustee replaced by the appointment of new trustees by the court.

---

6. PURPOSES OF A TRUST

INTRODUCTION

All trusts must have a purpose whether it be express or implied. Where a trust is set up in a trust deed it is usual for there to be an express clause stating the purposes which will be as per the requirements of the truster. There are some important limits on the purposes for which trusts can be set up. These include:

(a) purposes uncertain because of vagueness or lack of specification;

(b) purposes contrary to morality or public policy; and

(c) illegal purposes.

Uncertainty

If it cannot be determined what a truster wishes to be done with trust property the trust may be void for uncertainty. This uncertainty may arise in two ways:

(a) because the wording used by the truster is too vague; or

(b) because the trust purposes established by the truster are too wide.

Vagueness

Words used by a truster will usually be given their normal and everyday meaning and although such a meaning may not be absolutely fixed this will not normally render a trust purpose void for uncertainty. To ascertain the exact meaning the words used will be construed in the context of the whole deed and in certain circumstances this may differ from the normal everyday meaning. In addition certain terms may be given a fixed and certain meaning by statute. For example, the terms "children" or "issue" have been defined as including adopted and illegitimate children if used in the circumstances set out in the Law Reform (Miscellaneous Provisions) (Scotland) Act 1966, s. 5, the Law Reform (Miscellaneous Provisions) (Scotland) Act 1968, ss. 1–6 and the Law Reform (Parent and Child) (Scotland) Act 1986, s. 1(2).

Vagueness or ambiguity will render a trust purpose void only if it is of such a degree that the trust purposes cannot be determined from the words. For example, in *Hardie v. Morison* (1899) a trust was set up for the purposes of acquiring premises for the establishment of a bookshop for the sale of books dealing with the subjects of "free thought". The trust was held void for uncertainty because of the uncertain nature of the term "free thought".

Overly Wide Purposes

Trust purposes must be stated with sufficient certainty and precision and not so widely that they confer on the trustees such a wide discretion that it is the trustees' purposes which are being carried out and not those of the truster.

Broadly stated, it is quite competent for a truster to identify a class of persons and to confer on trustees the discretion to choose beneficiaries from within that class. By contrast, it is not competent for the truster to allow the trustees to select the class of persons. The distinction may not always be so clear-cut and will be a question of degree.

There are a few cases on this issue in relation to private trusts but the case law is somewhat difficult to reconcile.

(a) In *Sutherland's Trs v. Sutherland's Tr.* (1893) it was held that directions for distribution were void from uncertainty where they directed the trustees to distribute the trust assets "in such manner as they may think proper".

(b) In *Wood v. Wood's Exx* (1995) a will appointed an executrix and directed her to distribute the estate "as she knows I would wish it". This was held void from uncertainty and the estate fell into intestacy.

(c) A direction to pay to "those whom you know respect me" was upheld (*Warrender v. Anderson* (1893)). The judges in that case made the observation that the wording "those who respected me" (without any reference to the knowledge of the trustees) would have been bad because it gave no workable definition of the class of persons entitled.

(d) In *Macdonald v. Atherton* (1925) the court regarded as sufficiently precise a direction to benefit "nearest and most needful relatives on my mother's side".

Overly wide purposes can be a much greater problem with public trusts. The main area of difficulty is where the truster has specified a class of the general public who are intended to benefit.

(a) It has been held that a trust for "charities" or "charitable purposes" is sufficiently precise at least where trustees are appointed and given power to make the choice (*Angus's Exx v. Batchan's Trs* (1949)).

(b) In contrast to this stands the cases which have held that the expressions "public purposes" and "religious purposes" are too wide to be given effect to. See respectively *Blair v. Duncan* (1901) and *Rintoul's Trs v. Rintoul* (1949).

The problems may be exacerbated if the truster uses a list of adjectives disjunctively to widen the class of possible beneficiaries. For example, a class of "religious or public purposes" would appear to be wider than either "religious" purposes or "public" purposes when each of these is taken separately. By contrast one might suppose that if adjectives are used conjunctively the class would be narrowed. For example, a class of "religious and public purposes" would appear to cover only the overlap of "religious" purposes and "public" purposes. Unfortunately, language is not used as simply as that. For example:

(a) The word "and" may be used disjunctively rather than conjunctively. In *McConochie's Trs v. McConochie* (1909) a gift to "educational, charitable and religious purposes" was held void on the basis that the word "and" had been used disjunctively and this was confirmed by an instruction to divide the gift among these purposes.

(b) The word "or" may be used conjunctively rather than disjunctively or even exegetically to indicate that the next word explains the immediately preceding word. In *Wink's Exx v. Tallent* (1947) a trust was created for such "benevolent or charitable societies" as the trustee may choose. It was held that the trust was not void for uncertainty as the vague word "benevolent" was sufficiently explained or qualified by the subsequent word "charitable".

Contrary to morality
A trust purpose will be void if it is held by the court to be immoral or, otherwise stated, *contra bonos mores*.

Given the vast changes in society over the last few decades it may be difficult to apply the standards of morality identified last century. For example, earlier this century in England it was held that it was not illegal or contrary to morality to make a bequest to a company whose objects include a denial of Christianity (*Bowman v. Secular Society Limited* (1917)). It is difficult to see how this could ever be doubted today. Nevertheless some old moral standards may remain. A trust to further prostitution would probably still be immoral (see *Johnstone v. Mackenzie's Exrs* (1835)).

The courts will probably be reluctant to apply this ground of invalidity today.

Contrary to public policy
Trust purposes may not be contrary to public policy.

In the main the courts have restricted application of this doctrine to invalidate trust purposes that are so extravagant and wasteful that they are wholly lacking in benefit to the community. For example, in *Sutherland's Tr. v. Verschoyle* (1968) a truster purported to set up a trust to display what she believed was a valuable art collection. In fact it had little artistic value and the court held the purpose to be void on the basis that it was completely wasteful and contrary to public policy.

The main area of development for public policy in recent years has been trust purposes for extravagant funeral arrangements, tombstones and memorials. Only modest arrangements which conform to reasonable standards of decency and respects for the dead will be recognised (*McCaig v. Glasgow University* (1907); *McCaig's Trs v. Kirk Session of United Free Church of Lismore* (1915); *Aitken's Trs v. Aitken* (1927)).

Illegal purposes
A trust purpose must not be illegal. This can mean two separate things:

(a) The carrying out of the trust purpose must not foster a breach of the common law or criminal law such as would be the case if the trust benefited an illegal organisation; and
(b) The trust purpose must not be one which has been rendered incompetent by law. Examples of this form of illegality include entails and successive liferents and accumulations of income.

ENTAILS AND SUCCESSIVE LIFERENTS

An entail was a device which was used extensively up to the end of last century to avoid the dissipation of family assets. An entail worked by conveying property, such as a landed estate, to a party not as outright owner but as a trustee for future generations. When that party died and the property passed, as was usual, to the eldest son, that son, in turn, held the property in trust for future generations. The device was intended to continue in perpetuity. In relation to moveables, largely the same result could be achieved by the creation of a series of liferents with the fee vesting at some long-distant future time.

The great economic problem with entails and successive liferents was that they tied up land and valuable moveables and rendered them incapable of economic development.

Both of these devices have been considerably restricted by statute. The creation of new entails over land was prohibited by the Entails (Scotland) Act 1914 and successive liferents over moveables was restricted by the Trusts (Scotland) Act 1921, s. 9.

The modern legislative provision for both land and moveables is contained in the Law Reform (Miscellaneous Provisions) (Scotland) Act 1968, s. 18 which affects deeds executed after November 25, 1968. This provides that if a person, who was not living or *in utero* at the date of coming into operation of the deed creating the liferent, becomes entitled to that liferent, then on his attaining the age of majority (18 years of age) he shall own the property and not just a liferent therein. This effectively limits the endurance of the liferent to the minority of the person *in utero* (see *Stewart's Trs v. Whitelaw* (1926)).

The Scottish Law Commission has recommended that all land held under any existing entail should be automatically disentailed on an appointed day. (See *Scottish Law Commission, Report on the Abolition of the Feudal System*, No. 168, para. 9.17 and draft Bill, clauses 44–46).

ACCUMULATIONS OF INCOME — GENERAL

Accumulation is the continued reinvestment of income in such a way that the beneficial enjoyment of that income is postponed. Accumulation of income is commonly encountered in what are known as "accumulation and maintenance trusts" which are used to gather resources and then to expend them for purposes such as the maintenance of children or disabled parties. These types of trusts are quite legitimate and receive special treatment under taxation law.

Accumulation for very long periods or for indefinite periods could have detrimental economic effects and there are statutory limits to ensure that the postponement of the beneficial enjoyment of the income is limited in time. These statutory restrictions are now contained in the Trusts (Scotland) Act 1961, s. 5 and in the Law Reform (Miscellaneous Provisions) (Scotland) Act 1966, s. 6. These provisions apply to *mortis causa* and *inter vivos* trusts, to public and private trusts and they are retrospective.

It remains a theoretical possibility that a truster may avoid the rules on accumulation by choosing a legal system to govern the trust which does not prohibit accumulations. Such a choice may be made under the Recognition of Trusts Act 1987.

THE MODERN LAW ON ACCUMULATIONS

Provision is made against accumulation of the income of any property (including land) in whole or in part beyond any one of six specified periods as follows:

(a) the life of the granter;
(b) 21 years from the death of the granter;
(c) the minority of any person living or *in utero* at the date of the death of the grantor;
(d) the minority of any person who would, under the terms of the trust deed directing accumulation, be entitled to the income accumulated if of full age;
(e) 21 years from the making of the settlement or the other disposition; or
(f) the duration of the minority of any person living or *in utero* at the date of the making of the settlement or other disposition.

In respect of periods (c) and (d) minority is defined in the Trusts (Scotland) Act 1961, s. 5(6) as ending with the attainment of 21 years and so the Age of Majority (Scotland) Act 1969 does not apply to reduce the age to 18.

If accumulation is directed otherwise than as permitted, the direction is void and the income goes to the person who would have been entitled if there had been no direction to accumulate (Trusts (Scotland) Act 1961, s. 5(3)). This result is not usually what the truster would have intended. As a matter of good practice, the truster ought to be advised to consider all of these six time limitations and to ensure that one of them is expressly chosen. The trust deed ought to contain an express direction that there is no accumulation beyond that period.

The accumulation is not totally void if the period specified exceeds a period allowed, but is void as to the excess. This was applied in respect of limitation (b) noted above in *Carey's Trs v. Rose* (1957). A testator directed trustees to hold the residue of his estate until the son of his nephew attained 21 years of age. The will contained no directions about the income. The son was not born until two years after the death of the testator. The trustees accumulated the income until he was 21–23 years in total. It was clear that there had been illegal accumulations but unclear whether those entitled to the accumulations were entitled to the income generated in the first two or last two years. It was held that those entitled to the accumulations were entitled to the income generated in the last two years.

7. ADMINISTRATION OF THE TRUST

INTRODUCTION

After a trust is set up and the trustees have accepted office the trustees must commence the administration of the trust. The trustees will have a duty to carry out this administration, they will have certain powers to fulfil this duty and, in appropriate cases, considerable discretion in the exercise of those powers. In most cases they have a duty to exercise this discretion. Because of the interrelationship of the duties, powers and discretion these will be treated together.

The purposes of a trust will largely determine how it is to be administered. For example, more proactive administration is required where the trust is a public trust with charitable aims such as the running of a hospital as compared with a trust which is simply aimed at preserving investments until a single beneficiary reaches the age of majority. There are infinite variations between these extreme cases. As a result of this diversity, everything stated below must, of necessity, be no more than general guidance which will be applicable to most, but not all trusts.

There are three sources of the duties and powers of trustees. These are the trust deed, common law and statute. The duties in the trust deed will vary from case to case and each trust deed must be examined for its contents. As we shall see in chapter 10 a trustee has a general common law duty of care and all other common law and statutory duties may be regarded as specific applications or refinements of this general duty.

A TRUSTEE'S DUTY TO TAKE ADVICE BUT NOT TO DELEGATE

Once he has accepted office, a trustee must act personally and cannot generally delegate his duties either to another trustee or a third party. This is the application of the maxim *delegatus non potest delegare*. The maxim is a presumption rather than a general rule and it may be rebutted in appropriate circumstances.

A truster may make specific provision in the trust deed permitting trustees to delegate their duties or confirming that only one of a body of trustees will have exclusive responsibility for a specific specialist aspect of the trust estate.

Unless there is an express exclusion of the power in the trust deed, a trustee always has power to appoint agents when a person of reasonable prudence would do so (see *Leith v. East Coast Steam Shipping Co.* (1909)). For example, where a trust estate includes a house and it is the duty of the trustee to keep the house in good repair, the trustee need not paint it personally. He can employ reputable tradesmen to do this.

Not only has a trustee power to seek advice and assistance from appropriate parties but he has a duty to do so where this would be prudent. In some cases this common law duty is fortified by statute. For example, the Trustee Investments Act 1961, s. 6(2) requires a trustee to take advice on whether contemplated investments are suitable. The party from whom advice is sought must be someone reasonably believed by the trustees to be qualified by his ability in and practical experience in financial matters.

Under the Trusts (Scotland) Act 1921, s. 4(1)(f) a trustee is specifically given the power to appoint factors and law agents and to pay them suitable remuneration.

Although there is no doubt that all the trustees may collectively grant a power of attorney in favour of an agent so that an agent may execute deeds on the part of the trust, there remains a doubt as to whether a single trustee who is part of a number of trustees may delegate his authority to execute deeds on his behalf as a trustee leaving the others to sign personally. Whilst this doubt remains unresolved, conveyancers insist upon deeds being executed by all trustees personally.

OBLIGATION TO SECURE TRUST PROPERTY

A trustee has a duty to identify and ingather all trust property as soon as possible after taking up office. To do this a trustee has powers to implement this duty such as the right to call for the delivery of all trust property held by third parties. A classic example is a bank account in respect of which a trustee can call upon the bank for a statement of account. Where debts are due by third parties to the trust the trustees can raise a court action to recover the debt. Where new trustees are assumed they must recover all trust property in the hands of the former trustees.

This duty to ingather trust property is particularly important in respect of the position of an executor who has a duty to identify and ingather the whole of the executry estate. An executor is liable to be debited with the value of any estate which he fails to realise (see *Donald v. Hodgart's Trs* (1893)). In this case an engineer carried on a business with merchants in the Indian subcontinent. On his death the trustees failed to sell off the goodwill of this business. They took the view that the goodwill was personal to the engineer and thus disappeared when he died. They argued that there was nothing to sell. The court took a different view and ordered them to pay to the deceased's estate £300 as representing the value of the goodwill which they had failed to realise.

A trustee requires court authority not to ingather property (*Burns' C.B. v. Burns' Trs* (1961)). A *curator bonis* to a patient in a mental hospital sought authority from the court to elect on behalf of his ward either to accept the provisions in the will of the ward's deceased wife or to claim *jus relicti* out of her estate. Under the will the ward was given a legacy of £300. His *jus relicti* would have amounted to £26,000. He was aged 98, there was no possibility of recovery and he already had ample resources for his maintenance. The court permitted the *curator bonis* to elect the provisions under the will. This case has been applied in *B's C.B., Ptr* (1995) to permit a *curator bonis* to a ward aged 91 to renounce a large part of an inheritance due to his ward under her husband's estate. The ward was already well provided for and the effect of the renunciation was to mitigate the incidence of inheritance tax.

EXISTING DEBTS AND OBLIGATIONS

It is unusual for there to be outstanding debts and obligations at the start of the trust but there are two exceptional cases:

(a) *mortis causa* trusts where the purpose is to distribute the estate of the deceased to beneficiaries; and
(b) where the trust involves an existing business.

In respect of debts and obligations outstanding as at the date of commencement of the trust, the trustees are not personally liable for these debts but the trustees must pay them off or perform them as soon as possible after the trust estate has been ingathered. Only then can it be known whether the trust estate is solvent and only if it is solvent can the administration of the trust begin. If the trust estate is insolvent the trustees must come to an arrangement with the creditors, failing which any creditor to whom a debt of over £1,500 is owed (or a majority of the trustees with the consent of such a creditor) may petition for the sequestration of the estate of a deceased debtor or the trust (Bankruptcy (Scotland) Act 1985, ss. 5(3) and (6)).

In the case of testamentary trusts the trustees usually wait six months after the death of the debtor before paying any debts (except privileged debts such as funeral expenses which can be paid immediately) to allow creditors to lodge claims. The trustees cannot be compelled to pay an ordinary debt until the expiry of six months from the date of death (Act of Sederunt of February 28, 1662). The executors' duty to pay out to beneficiaries must be limited by their obligation to pay debts of the deceased first. Executors may pay out only when the estate is solvent. If they pay out of an insolvent estate the trustees will be liable to the creditors. See, for example, *Murray's Trustees v. Murray* (1905). In this case testamentary trustees handed over a piano, the subject of a specific bequest, to the beneficiary. The trust estate turned out to be insolvent and the trustees were held liable to account to the creditors for the value of the piano.

NEW DEBTS AND OBLIGATIONS

The trust may incur new debts in the course of the administration of the trust and in respect of these debts the trustees assume personal liability unless they expressly contract to the contrary. This is simply one aspect of the general rule which imposes on trustees personal liability in respect of obligations in contracts entered into by them. This general rule will be examined at p. 68.

A trustee is entitled to be indemnified out of the trust estate in respect of debts properly incurred by him in the course of trust administration.

In some trust deeds which set up continuing trusts the truster will seek to impose some permanent control upon the level of debt which may be incurred by the trustees in a given period. For example, the trust deed may provide that the ratio of debt incurred by the trustees may not exceed a certain proportion of the valuation of all the trust property. A trustee who incurs debt beyond the permitted limit will be in breach of trust and will not be entitled to be indemnified out of the trust estate in the usual manner.

DUTY TO KEEP ACCOUNTS

Except in exceptional cases, a trustee has a common law duty to keep accounts to show their intromissions with the trust estate (*Polland v. Sturrock's Exrs* (1955)). The accounts should show the amounts spent, the persons to whom payment was made, the nature of the payment and they must be supported by the appropriate vouchers. It is only by keeping accounts that a trustee can show that he has paid over to a beneficiary all that is due to him less all properly incurred expenditure. Without such proof in the form of accounts a trustee may be found liable for gross neglect (*Wilson v. Guthrie Smith* (1894)).

An exceptional case occurred in *Leitch v. Leitch* (1927). A farmer died leaving a wife with a large family. The farmer's father assigned to the widow the lease of the farm "for behoof of herself and her family". The widow continued to live on the farm and brought up the family there. Years later one of the children raised an action for accounting. The court dismissed the action and held that in the special familial circumstances it was clear that the truster did not impose on the trustee any duty to keep accounts.

In some circumstances the common law rule has been supplemented by statutory rules to ensure that the accounts comply with particular requirements. For example, in terms of the Bankruptcy (Scotland) Act 1985, s.3(1)(f) the permanent trustee is obliged to keep regular accounts of his intromissions with the debtor's estate.

DUTY TO PAY THE CORRECT BENEFICIARIES

A trustee is under a duty to pay to the correct beneficiaries and may be liable to the true beneficiary if an incorrect payment is made.

This also means that a trustee is under a duty to establish who are the correct beneficiaries. To do this he must usually familiarise himself with the trust deed.

The duty extends to an obligation to pay the correct beneficiaries at the proper time. If beneficiaries are not paid at the correct time the trustees will be liable to pay interest from the date the estate should have been distributed or to make up any depreciation the estate has suffered since that date (*Cross v. Cross' Trs* (1919)).

Where trustees are given discretion as to when to pay out the trust estate to beneficiaries they must exercise their discretion reasonably.

LIABILITY FOR IMPROPER DISTRIBUTION

If trustees pay to incorrect beneficiaries they are normally liable to the person who should have received the payment whether he be a beneficiary or a creditor.

The liability of the trustees in this regard appears to be strict liability rather than a liability based on what the prudent trustee would have done. This is justified on the basis that if they are in doubt it is open to the trustees to require those claiming to be beneficiaries to prove their entitlement and, if they are still in doubt, to petition the court for directions.

If there is any doubt over a beneficiary's entitlement the trustees should withhold payment. When a woman became entitled to income from a trust when she obtained a decree of divorce it was held that the trustees should have ceased to make payment to her when the former husband's trustee in bankruptcy raised an action for reduction of the divorce decree which was ultimately successful (*Corebridge v. Fraser* (1915).

EXCEPTIONS TO LIABILITY FOR IMPROPER DISTRIBUTION

There are a number of circumstances in which trustees will not be liable to pay to the correct beneficiaries if they have already paid out to the wrong beneficiaries. These are as:

(1) where the trustees make a mistake in foreign law. For this purpose foreign law includes the law of Northern Ireland and the law of England;
(2) where the trustees have paid to someone who is apparently entitled but who has, without intimating the assignation, assigned their right to a third party. If intimation of the assignation is received by the trustees this exception ceases to exist in respect of the relevant assignation;
(3) where the incorrect payment is made because of the fault of the true beneficiary. In that case that beneficiary may be personally barred from pursuing the trustees for payment;
(4) where the trust estate has been stolen or embezzled by a third party in circumstances where the trustees were not negligent and it is no longer in the possession of the trustees;
(5) there is a speciality in respect of illegitimate children in terms of the Law Reform (Miscellaneous Provisions) (Scotland) Act 1968, s. 7 as

amended by the Law Reform (Parent & Child) (Scotland) Act 1986. An executor or trustee may distribute the estate without having ascertained that no illegitimate person or a paternal relative of such a person is entitled to an interest therein. The executor is not liable to any person so entitled of whose claim he has not had notice at the time of distribution. However, the right of the person so entitled to recover the payment or property from the person who has received it is not affected by this provision;

(6) where the trustee has acted honestly and reasonably and the court considers that he ought fairly to be excused in terms of the Trusts (Scotland) Act 1921, s. 32 (see pp. 66–67).

RECOVERY OF PAYMENTS AFTER IMPROPER DISTRIBUTION

If trust property has been handed over to the wrong person the trustees can demand return and payment thereof but only if incorrect payment by the trustees is based on an error of fact and not of law. The type of action required is known as a *condictio indebiti*.

A mistake of identity is an error of fact but a mistake in interpreting a trust deed is an error of law. In *Grant v. Grant's Exrs* (1994) trustees misinterpreted the provisions of a will and paid the wrong beneficiaries. They then tried to recover the sums from the parties to whom the incorrect payment had been made. It was held they could not do so as their error had been one of law and not fact.

Where heritable property in respect of which a Land Registered title exists is recovered by trustees from a person to whom the trust property should not have been paid that party cannot recover under the statutory indemnity of the Keeper (Land Registration (Scotland) Act 1979, s. 12(3)(j)(ii)).

INVESTMENT POWERS, DUTIES AND DISCRETION

These are dealt with in chapter 8.

POWERS OF TRUSTEES

The powers of trustees are derived from three sources:

(a) the trust deed;
(b) statute; and
(c) the common law.

POWERS GRANTED IN THE TRUST DEED

Each trust deed is different and a truster should confer on his trustees powers which are suitable to the purposes for which the trust is set up. In each case the trust deed must be examined to determine what are the powers of the trustees.

The trust deed may confer a specific power on the trustees expressly or by implication. They will be implied only if the powers are necessary for the achievement for the specified purposes of the trust. In rare cases the trust deed will expressly exclude certain powers from the range of powers available to the trustees.

Many trust deeds dating from last century contain a long list of powers available to trustees but these are rare in modern trust deeds as such lists have been largely superseded by statute.

POWERS CONFERRED BY STATUTORY PROVISIONS

The terms of each statutory power must be examined to determine its extent but they may be classified in the following ways:

(a) provisions limited to certain types of trustees;
(b) provisions limited to certain powers conferred without court application; and
(c) provisions limited to certain powers conferred only upon court application.

Statutory provisions limited to certain trustees

Under certain statutes some trustees have special additional powers to enable them to carry out their functions but these have no relevance to trustees generally. For example:

(1) A permanent trustee has many special powers in terms of the Bankruptcy (Scotland) Act 1985 including powers to challenge gratuitous alienations of the debtor, special rights of access to the documents and business affairs of the debtor and rights to adopt contracts entered into by the debtor; and

(2) In terms of the Judicial Factors Act 1849, s. 7 a judicial factor may apply to the court for certain special powers. It was judicially confirmed in *Bell's C.B., Noter* (1999) that, when read together with the terms of the Children Act 1995, s.10; 1849 Act, s.7 conferred on a *curator bonis* to a mentally disabled child, in appropriate cases and subject to the approval of the court, powers to invest all or part of the estate in an annuity. This power is not affected by any of the provisions of the Trustee Investments Act 1961.

(3) In terms of the Married Women's Policies of Assurance (Scotland) Act 1880, s. 2(2) the trustee in respect of the relevant policy of assurance has the following additional powers if the acts are not at variance with the terms or purposes of the trust:
    (a) to exercise any option under the policy, or under any deed of trust or other document constituting a trust in relation to the policy;
    (b) to convert the policy to a partially or a fully paid-up assurance;
    (c) to convert the policy into any other form of assurance on the life of the person effecting the policy;

(d) to increase or reduce the amount of the annual premiums payable under the policy;
(e) to alter the period during which the premiums under the policy are payable; and
(f) to surrender the policy.

Statutory powers without court application

The Trusts (Scotland) Act 1921, s. 4 contains 17 general powers of trustees where such acts are not at variance with the terms or purposes of the trust. For the full list, reference should be made to the Act itself. The first six of these powers are broadly speaking as follows:

(a) the power to sell trust estate;
(b) the power to feu trust estate. (This power will cease to be exercisable upon the abolition of the feudal system in implement of the *Scottish Law Commission, Report on the Abolition of the Feudal System,* No. 168, para. 2.8 and draft Bill, clause 2(3));
(c) the power to grant leases;
(d) the power to borrow money on the security of the trust estate;
(e) the power to excamb any part of the trust estate; and
(f) the power to acquire with trust funds a residence for any of the beneficiaries.

The list does not permit the trustees to do anything they wish and the following two "missing" powers should be noted:

(a) There is no express power to grant servitudes over trust property although this may be implied in some cases where it is consonant with the purposes of the trust. Frequently there will be no express power to this effect in the trust deed; and
(b) The only power to purchase heritage is limited to the power to acquire with trust funds a residence for any of the beneficiaries. If trustees wish to purchase any other form of heritage they must rely on the terms of the trust deed or exceptionally on the common law.

The 17 general powers of trustees will not be implied where such acts are "at variance with the terms or purposes of the trust". This is a twofold test. The "terms" of the trust are the actual words used by the truster himself — if a power is expressly excluded in the trust deed it cannot be implied by the 1921 Act, s. 4. The "purposes" of the trust relates to the specified aims or the ultimate aim of the trust.

The words "at variance" used in the 1921 Act, s. 4 do not require it to be shown that the power is absolutely necessary for the trust. A power will not be "at variance" with the terms or provisions of the trust if it is merely useful for the achievement of the aims of the trust.

In terms of the Trusts (Scotland) Act 1961, s. 2(1) where the trustees enter into a transaction with a third party involving acts under any of the six heads listed above the validity of the transaction cannot be challenged by the third party on the ground that the act in question is at variance with the terms of the trust or purposes of the trust.

In terms of the Lands Clauses Consolidation (Scotland) Act 1845, s. 7 a trustee has power to sell land forming part of a trust estate in a voluntary sale to promoters of an undertaking who possess compulsory purchase powers even though the trustees are otherwise disabled from doing so.

Statutory powers with court application

The 1921 Act, s. 16 enables the court to authorise trustees to make advances from the capital of a fund destined absolutely or contingently to beneficiaries who at the date of the application to the court are not yet of full age. But the scope of the section is limited by the requirements that the advance must be necessary for the maintenance or education of the beneficiaries, that it is not expressly prohibited by the trust deed and that the rights of the beneficiaries, if contingent, are contingent only on their survivance.

The Trusts (Scotland) Act 1921, s. 5 permits the court on the petition of the trustees to grant authority to them to do any of the acts mentioned in the 1921 Act, s. 4 (which sets out the general powers of trustees), notwithstanding that such an act is at variance with the terms or purposes of the trust, on being satisfied that such act is in all the circumstances expedient for the execution of the trust.

The 1921 Act, s. 5 imposes a single test which requires to be satisfied before the court will grant the power requested. The petitioners must show that the act is in all the circumstances "expedient for the execution of the trust". It will only be in unusual circumstances where the power sought would fail this test but this occurred in *Conage's J.F.* (1948). A judicial factor sought permission to sell the heritable property of a trust. The court refused to grant the power because one of the aims of the trust was to preserve the property as a family estate. In many more cases petitions are refused not because the court refuses to grant the power sought but because the courts take the view that the trustees have the power already and the petition is unnecessary. Only in clearly frivolous cases would the courts award expenses against the trustees personally and such petitions are generally regarded as useful in that they give the trustees a measure of security.

A petition under the 1921 Act, s. 5 is appropriate in relation to both public and private trusts. Hence it may be determined by the court pending a decision on whether the trust is either a public or a private trust and whether it is appropriate to sanction a variation under a *cy-près* scheme or in terms of the Law Reform (Miscellaneous Provisions) (Scotland) Act 1990, ss. 9 and 10. For example, in *Tod's Trs, Ptrs* (1999) the trustees under a trust set up to hold a large country house for the purpose of providing professional persons with rest and a change of air petitioned the court for power to sell the property. This was granted before determination of whether the trust was a public or private trust because the condition of the property was deteriorating and the trust estate would lose value if the sale was delayed.

Under the Trusts (Scotland) Act 1961, s. 1 the court may approve an arrangement for the variation of trust purposes. This provision will be examined in more detail at pp. 76–78. In certain circumstances the variation of trust purposes sought in terms of this provision may involve the conferring upon the trustees of powers to which they would not otherwise be entitled (whether under the trust deed or any other statutory provision). For example, it has been held that the 1961 Act, s. 1 may be invoked to extend the limitations on powers of investment contained in the Trustee Investments Act 1961 (see *Henderson, Ptr* (1981)).

POWERS CONFERRED AT COMMON LAW

In rare cases the trustees may obtain an additional power by petitioning the *nobile officium* of the Court of Session. This is an equitable jurisdiction of last resort and the additional power will be granted at the discretion of the court and not on demand.

The few decided cases which exist indicate that the court will exercise its discretion only in exceptional cases where a power is unavailable under the trust deed and cannot be obtained by any statutory provision. For example, in *Anderson's Trs* (1921) the court granted authority to trustees to purchase a particular item of heritage even though they had no power to do so in the trust deed or under the 1921 Act, s. 4. The item of heritage in question was the landlord's interest in the lease of a farm held by the trust as tenants. The purpose of the trust was to maintain the farm until the truster's nephew reached adulthood and could run the farm himself. The landlord had offered to sell the farm to the trust and a failure to take up the offer could have destroyed the purposes of the trust. In granting the power to purchase the farm the court emphasised the exceptional nature of the case and confirmed that it could not be used as a precedent.

DECISION MAKING

The decision making mechanism of a trust involves four issues as follows:

(a) who is to be consulted?
(b) what constitutes a quorum of trustees?
(c) when is majority decision making permitted?
(d) who can exercise and supervise discretion?

Consultation
In all decisions relating to the trust administration all trustees have a right to be consulted and a majority of trustees cannot exclude the participation of a minority in the administration of the trust.

In some rare cases, however, a trustee, by his own actions, may indicate that he has foregone his right to be consulted. In *Malcolm v. Goldie* (1895) one of a number of trustees had emigrated to Australia without resigning from office. The remaining trustees did not consult him when they assumed new trustees. Some years later this assumption was challenged on the basis of lack of consultation with the trustee who had emigrated. It was held that the assumption was valid and that the duty to consult extended only to reasonable consultation. The majority of the trustees were not obliged to obtain the input of a trustee to decision making if that trustee had made himself inaccessible.

What is a quorum?
The administration of the trust may continue only for so long as a quorum of trustees participates.

The truster may specify what constitutes a quorum in the trust deed. This is usually a majority of trustees but it may be less or more. If a certain number is specified as a quorum and the total number of trustees falls below this number the quorum becomes inoperative and the trust administration may be continued with the lesser number of trustees.

In rare circumstances, a truster may specify that he has appointed a *sine qua non* trustee. This is a trustee who must participate in trust administration before it can be undertaken.

If nothing is stated in the trust deed the Trusts (Scotland) Act 1921, s. 3(c) provides that a majority of the trustees accepting and surviving shall be a quorum.

Majority decisions
Acts of trust administration may be undertaken by a majority of trustees except in the rare case where the appointment of trustees is stated in the trust deed to be "joint". Thus, in the normal case a minority of trustees have no veto on acts of trust administration.

Because a majority of trustees can overrule the minority this means that they may impose liability on the whole body of trustees. The minority cannot prevent this but if they wish to avoid the liability they may resign as trustees. Only in rare cases, where the majority of trustees are acting in breach of trust or in bad faith will the minority of trustees be able to petition the court to have the acts of the majority interdicted. For example in *Reid v. Maxwell* (1852) a minority of trustees were held entitled to petition the court to prevent the majority assuming new trustees in an underhand way.

There are a number of examples of statutory provisions which have a bearing on acts of administration of trust business by a majority of trustees. One of the most important is the Bankruptcy (Scotland) Act 1985, s. 6(3) which provides that if the trust estate is insolvent a majority of the trustees with the consent of any creditor to whom a debt of over £1,500 is owed may petition for the sequestration of the estate of the trust.

There is some doubt as to whether the common law rule concerning majority decisions and any statutory variation of this extends to acts of administration or conveyancing in relation to heritable property. Although much may be said either way, in practice no conveyancing transaction involving a trust will be settled by a purchaser until all the trustees execute the relevant disposition.

Interference by the courts in the discretion of trustees
As a general rule the courts will not readily interfere with the discretion of trustees. The courts take the view that the trustees are in the best position to make proper judgments in relation to trust circumstances. For example

in *Brown v. Elder's Trs* (1906) the court refused to interfere in the exercise of the trustees' discretion because to do so would amount to the substitution of the court's judgment for that of the trustees who had been appointed by the truster for the very purpose of exercising that discretion.

Only in cases where the improper exercise of a discretion or the failure to exercise a discretion amounts to a breach of trust or is clearly unreasonable will the courts interfere. It may be difficult to decide when judicial interference is appropriate as is demonstrated by two contrasting cases:

(a) In *Chivas' Trs v. Stewart* (1907) trustees were given power to set aside a sum of such size as they thought fit for the payment of an annuity to a beneficiary. They set aside a very generous sum but the court held that it was not so large as to permit the courts to set aside the exercise of the trustees' discretion on the basis that it was unreasonable.

(b) In *Thomson v. Davidson's Trs* (1888) the trustees were instructed to provide financial relief for the truster's descendants. They offered 12 shillings and sixpence (62.5p) per week to a widow and six children. The court held that this was wholly inadequate and directed the trustees to pay the widow an annual sum of £10 per child.

In some cases the courts may find it appropriate to indicate that the trustees should exercise their discretion but will not intervene to require how that discretion should be exercised except to insist that the exercise is reasonable. For example, in *Ross v. Governors of Heriot's Hospital* (1843) the court declared that a certain individual fell within the class of persons out of which the trustees could select individuals upon whom to bestow benefits. Nevertheless, the court declined to require the trustees to bestow the benefit on a particular individual who fell within that class.

In certain special statutory circumstances judicial interference in the exercise of a trustee's discretion is made possible at the invitation of the trustee. For example in terms of the Bankruptcy (Scotland) Act 1985, s.3(6) the permanent trustee may apply to the sheriff for directions in relation to any particular matter arising in relation to the sequestration. In addition persons known as commissioners may be elected under the Bankruptcy (Scotland) Act 1985, s. 4 to supervise the intromissions of the permanent trustee and to advise him.

Who may exercise discretionary powers?

Any party who is a trustee, no matter how appointed — whether by the truster or by the court — is entitled to exercise discretion provided it is in relation to administrative matters (*Angus's Exx v. Batchan's Trs* (1949)).

Where, however, the discretion is of a dispositive nature — discretion that affects the nature or extent of the beneficiary's interest — not everyone can exercise this discretion. Two judicial approaches to this matter may be noted:

(a) In *Robbie's J.F. v. Macrae* (1893) a testatrix instructed her executors to pay sums to such charitable purposes as they thought proper. The executors died before they could make the choice and the court appointed a judicial factor to the estate. It was held that the right to choose the charities entitled to receive the sums was personal to the trustees originally appointed by the truster and this choice could not be made by the judicial factor. In the later case of *Russell's Ex v. Balden* (1989) this earlier case was explained by Lord Jauncey as being decided on the basis that only those persons who take their authority from the truster and not the court can exercise dispositive discretion.

(b) A different approach — but one which in the circumstances achieved the same results — is to be seen in *Angus's Exx v. Batchan's Trs* (1949). A will provided that certain sums were to be paid to "charities". No trustee or executor was appointed. It was held that the gift was void from uncertainty and the court had no power to appoint a judicial factor who could exercise the discretion. The basis of the discretion was the doctrine of *delectus personae*. It was presumed that only persons chosen by the truster could be aware of the truster's wishes and could implement them in the exercise of dispositive discretion.

The different legal approaches may reach different results in relation to trustees appointed by the court under the Trusts (Scotland) Act 1921, s. 22. It was assumed in *Angus's Exx v. Batchan's Trs* (1949) that such parties would have the power to exercise dispositive discretion but since trustees appointed in terms of the 1921 Act, s. 22 are not chosen by the truster this is inconsistent with the view that only those benefiting from *delectus personae* benefit from such discretion. By contrast, such parties appointed in terms of the 1921 Act, s.22 are trustees and not judicial factors and can be regarded as being in the same position as trustees nominated by the truster. There is therefore no illogicality in holding that they are entitled to exercise dispositive discretion.

---

8. INVESTMENT DUTIES OF A TRUSTEE

INTRODUCTION

Where trustees hold the trust estate for any longer than a minimal period they will have a duty to use it in a manner which protects its value in real terms. Except in the rare cases where this can be achieved by merely preserving the trust property before passing it on to the beneficiaries this will entail investment which complies with three requirements:

(a) the interest of no beneficiary is to be exposed to greater risk than any other;
(b) any investment must be "authorised"; and
(c) any investment must be "proper".

All three of these requirements relate to risk management in various ways:—

(a) The first is to ensure fairness amongst all beneficiaries.
(b) The second permits the truster to set out in advance of a trust being set up a framework specifying certain limitations on the type of investments which can be made by trustees and the appropriate mix of those investments. If the truster fails to do so a statutory framework of authorised investments will apply in terms of the Trustee Investments Act 1961.
(c) The third requires the trustees to assess the appropriateness of any investments not only upon initial investment but also from time to time in the light of the risks and benefits to the trust.

EQUALISATION OF RISKS — APPROPRIATION OF INVESTMENTS

Because the interest of no beneficiary is to be exposed to greater risk than any other this means that all the beneficiaries are entitled to have their interests secured by the whole trust fund and the trustees will have no power to appropriate particular investments to particular beneficiaries except where:

(a) the truster directs otherwise in the trust deed either expressly or impliedly; or,
(b) all the beneficiaries consent to the appropriation.

In some cases the power to appropriate may be implied from the terms of the provisions stated in the trust deed. For example, if the truster directs that a part of the estate is to be distributed immediately to certain beneficiaries with the remainder not being distributed until a later date this infers an appropriation of the parts of the estate otherwise the beneficiaries to be paid first would not be aware of the value of their entitlements until the remainder of the estate was realised.

Once an appropriation is intimated to the beneficiaries it is irrevocable unless the power to reappropriate is reserved by the truster in the trust deed or a reappropriation is consented to by all the beneficiaries.

AUTHORISED INVESTMENTS

A trustee is limited in the type of investments he can choose. These limitations derive from two main sources:

(a) the common law as amended by statute; and
(b) the provisions of the trust deed.

At common law a trustee was limited to investing in British government consolidated stock or loans or on heritable security. This was considered too restrictive because although it provided absolute security the meagre return was outstripped by inflation. The common law has been amended by statute on a number of occasions most recently by the Trustee Investments Act 1961.

The powers of investment in the Trustee Investments Act 1961 are without prejudice to any provision in a trust deed (1961 Act, s. 3(1)). This means that if nothing is stated in the trust deed then the common law as amended by statute applies. By contrast, if express provision was made in the trust deed that provision will be enforced but will be strictly construed, especially if it permits investments which are wider than those permitted under the general law.

STRUCTURE OF THE TRUSTEE INVESTMENTS ACT 1961

The 1961 Act deals with investment by trustees and not investment by the truster. Where the trust estate originally passed to the trustees includes investments these will not be covered by the 1961 Act as it was the truster and not the trustees who made the investments. In such a case the trustees need not sell and re-invest in accordance with the provisions of the 1961 Act.

The provisions of the 1961 Act may be split into three types:

(a) those relating to types of authorised investments;
(b) those requiring a balanced mix of investments; and
(c) those relating to duties falling upon trustees in deciding whether a particular investment is proper.

Types of investment authorised under the 1961 Act
The framework of the 1961 Act is centred on the classification of investments under the 1961 Act, Sched. 1.

In this schedule investments are divided into three categories as follows:

(a) Part I of Sched. 1 of the 1961 Act lists "narrower range investments not requiring advice". These are the least risky investment such as national savings certificates.
(b) Part II of the Schedule lists "narrower range investments requiring advice". These are slightly more risky but generally secure investments such as heritable securities, UK company debentures and government securities.
(c) Part III of the schedule lists "wider range investments". These are the most risky of the three types of authorised investment and were not permitted before the passing of the 1961 Act. Part III includes shares in building societies, units in Unit Trust schemes and shares in certain companies.

Not all companies qualify and in terms of the 1961 Act, Sched. 1, Pts III and IV trustees may invest only in a company which complies with certain requirements. Broadly speaking, this limits investment to U.K. companies which are quite large and who have been successful in recent years. The requirements for a suitable company are as follows:

(a) it must be incorporated in the U.K.;
(b) it must be quoted on the stock exchange;
(c) its shares must be fully paid up or required to be fully paid up within nine months of the issue;
(d) it must have a total paid up share capital of not less than £1 million; and
(e) it must have paid a dividend on all its shares entitled to rank for a dividend in each of the preceding five years.

If the provisions of the 1961 Act apply to a trust, a trustee cannot invest in any investment of a type which is not listed in the Schedule. For example:

(a) Nothing in the 1961 Act permits a trustee to invest in a purchase of land or buildings. A common additional investment power is a power to purchase heritage. If this is not stated in the trust deed the trustees will have only a limited power to purchase heritage as a residence for any of the beneficiaries in terms of the Trusts (Scotland) Act 1921, s. 4(1)(ee).
(b) Nothing in the 1961 Act permits a trustee to invest in small unquoted companies such as family companies. Again, if the truster wishes the trustees to have this power he must make specific provision to this effect.
(c) Nothing in the 1961 Act permits a trustee to invest in life assurance policies. Again, if the truster wishes the trustees to have this power he must make specific provision to this effect.

Mix of investment required under the 1961 Act

Where the 1961 Act applies it is not sufficient to enable investment in a particular type of investment for the trustee to show that it falls within the three classes in the Schedule. In addition, for a trustee to invest he must show that overall he has achieved the correct mix of investments. The special rules for achieving the right mix of investments are principally contained in the Trustee Investments Act 1961, s. 2.

Chief amongst these rules is the rule that where a trustee wishes to invest in wider range investments he must divide the whole trust fund into two parts which (until 1996) were required to be equal in value at the time of division and only invest one half in the "wider-range part" and one half in the "narrower-range part". This proportion of each fund to the other has now been amended by Trustee Investments (Division of Trust Fund) Order 1996 S.I. 1996 No. 845. This came into force on May 11, 1996. The statutory instrument permits the wider range fund to be up to three times as large as the narrow range fund.

If the trustees do not wish to invest in wider range investments, they do not need to split the fund.

Once the split has been made the parts are to be administered as if they were two separate funds. Nevertheless, 1961 Act, s.2(4) provides that where property is to be taken out of the trust fund, the trustees have a discretion in relation to the property taken out. This has the consequence that current drawings or payments or distributions to beneficiaries may, if the trustees so wish, be made from the narrow range fund until that is used up completely, leaving only the wider range fund.

Once the fund is split it may not be split again and assets may not be transferred from one part to another unless a compensating transfer of the same value is made into the fund out of which the assets were transferred. If new property is acquired by the trust this must also be split between the two parts or placed in one with a compensating transfer to the other (1961 Act, s. 2(3)). Nevertheless any income arising or capital appreciation generated by the property in one part is to be treated as belonging solely to that part and no compensating transfer is required to keep the two parts in original parity of size. As a result, the relative value of the two funds may become completely out of step with the original proportions.

Before making any split the trustees must value the property. In terms of the 1961 Act, s.5(1) if they obtain a valuation in writing from a person reasonably believed to be qualified to make it, such valuation shall be conclusive in determining whether the split has been properly made.

THE SPECIAL DIRECTIONS OF THE TRUSTER

It is open to the truster to provide for powers of investment in the trust deed which differ from those allowed under the Trustee Investments Act 1961. He may waive the requirements of the Act in whole or in part or provide an entirely new scheme of investment. If the requirements of the 1961 Act are waived in whole or in part and a wholly new scheme of investment substituted therefor the whole terms of the statutory authorisation of investments under the 1961 Act, s. 1 may be disregarded.

Where the truster specifies that the trust is to invest in certain investments which would not be authorised under the scheme of the 1961 Act these are to be put into a separate fund and are known as "special-range property" (1961 Act, s. 3 and Sched. 2). If the whole of the trust property is comprised in the special-range property the terms of the 1961 Act do not apply. If not all of the trust property is comprised in the special-range property, the balance of the trust property is split up into funds according to the scheme of the 1961 Act.

It is possible for the trust deed to provide that the trustees will have narrower powers of investment than those provided for in the 1961 Act. An example of this may occur where the truster requires the trustees to avoid investments in what the truster regards as unethical investments such as companies manufacturing cigarettes or alcohol.

It is common for modern trust deeds to provide that the trustees will have wider powers of investment than those provided for in the 1961 Act. If this is what the truster wishes he should do so expressly and unambiguously. Any ambiguity in the wording used will be resolved in favour of the security of trust funds as was exemplified in *Moss's Trs v. King* (1952). A trust deed granted to trustees "the fullest powers … of investment". It was held that this clause did not grant the trustees the fullest powers which an unrestricted owner would have but only such powers of investment as would be granted by the common law to a party under fiduciary duty like a trustee. If such a clause were to be used today the prudent course is to assume that such a trustee would still be bound by the provisions of the 1961 Act.

If a truster confers on trustees wider powers of investment than would be permitted under the general law these wider powers will not transmit to a judicial factor appointed to the trust estate (*Carmichael's J.F.* (1971)) but they will transmit to a *curator bonis* who administers the estate on behalf of an *incapax* at least insofar as this relates to retaining the ward's investments as compared to making new investments (*Fraser v. Paterson (No. 2)* 1988)). The difference lies in the element of *delectus personae* involved in the selection of trustees. A judicial factor takes his authority on behalf of the court not the truster. By contrast, a *curator bonis* acts on behalf of the *incapax*.

PERMITTED AND PROPER INVESTMENTS

A trustee has a general duty only to make "proper" investments. "Authorised" investments (*i.e.* those permitted by statute or in the trust deed) are not necessarily "proper" investments. Broadly speaking, a proper investment is one which is authorised but which provides a suitable return for the trust without exposing the trust to excessive risk.

Difficulties arise where there is argument that provisions in the trust deed not only authorise a type of investment but confirm that it is proper in some or all circumstances. The courts are reluctant to accept that this is the case and the position may be summarised in three propositions as follows:

(a) An investment which is proper in a given economic climate may be unsuitable in another even though the trustee is expressly authorised to invest in that type of investment either in terms of the trust deed or by statute.

(b) Where the trust estate originally passed to the trust includes investments purchased by the truster this does not absolve the trustees of their duty to review the investments from time to time and decide whether the investments are still "proper" and if the original investments are to be sold or retained. For example, in *Clarke v. Clarke's Trs* (1925) the trustees were authorised to retain investments which the truster had made. The shares gradually lost their value and the trustees were held liable to the beneficiaries because they had not reviewed the investments.

(c) Even where the trust deed prohibits the trustees from selling certain investments originally acquired by the truster, this may not be sufficient to absolve the trustees of a duty to re-assess those investments from time to time. This means that in certain cases it may even be the duty of the trustees to sell a failing investment in the face of an express prohibition to do so. They may do this even without court authorisation under the Trusts (Scotland) Act 1921, s. 5 or the Trusts (Scotland) Act 1961, s. 1.

What is a proper investment?
A trustee has a duty of care to the beneficiaries to make only "proper" investments. This common law standard of care is the same standard of the ordinary prudent trustee that is applied in respect of all other aspects of trust management (see further at pp. 60 and 61). The common law duty of care is re-stated in the Trustee Investments Act 1961, s. 6 where it is applied to various aspects of investment.

When investing a trustee is required to have regard to the need for diversification of the investments of the trust in so far as is appropriate to the circumstances of the trust (1961 Act, s. 6(1)(a)). This is an obligation on the trustee to consider the risks of having all his eggs in one basket. If the trustee invests in one project the risk is that this might fail and the trust will lose everything. This does not preclude investment in one asset only provided this is appropriate to the circumstances of the trust.

When investing a trustee is required to have regard to the suitability of the investments (1961 Act, s. 6(1)(b)). This obligation requires the trustee to consider the nature of the trust in comparison with the nature of the investment. There are innumerable variants which may occur in practice but the following serve to illustrate the matter:

(a) A trust which has long term objectives will probably require investments which have a potential for long term growth. If the trust, by contrast, is for a purpose where income is required immediately, the trustee will not find suitable investments in shares which give capital growth only.

(b) Where the purposes of the trust are merely to preserve the value of the estate a more conservative investment strategy may be appropriate as compared to a case where a the purposes of the trust are to achieve a particular object such as the provision of venture capital for start-up businesses.

(c) In making proper investments a trustee will require to make a balanced selection of investments generating capital appreciation as well as income where there are various beneficiaries, some with an interest in the capital and others with interests in the income.

(d) It is possible to argue that "suitability" extends beyond merely financial criteria. It may be the case that investment in particular businesses may be unsuitable in certain cases. For example, if a trust is set up to promote the purposes of a religious group or churches which promote pacifism then investment in companies manufacturing arms or explosives may be unsuitable.

Where the trustee makes an investment he cannot simply leave it there. He is obliged by the 1961 Act, s.6(3) from time to time to reconsider whether that investment is still appropriate. The regularity of this consideration obviously depends on the nature of the investment. If shares in a blue chip company are purchased and the market for that company's products are strong and their share price stable then the interval of reappraisal of the suitability of the investments is likely to be much longer than another company with a more volatile track record.

"Proper investments" — balance of risk and security

All investments involve some degree of risk. The duty to invest properly means that the trustee must take some risk. Although he must take some risk, a trustee has a duty not to take excessive risk and he generally cannot invest in speculative ventures. The trustee must achieve a proper balance between risk and security. This amounts to a duty of care owed by the trustee to the beneficiaries. Where the trustee fails to invest properly he will be liable to account to the beneficiaries for the income that the estate, properly invested, would have generated.

Where trust property includes money the trustee cannot simply take no risks at all as would be the case if he buried it in the ground for safety. (*viz.* the parable of the talents in *Matthew*, Chap. 25, vv. 14–30). Instead the trustee has a duty to invest the money to earn interest for the trust. However, it is not sufficient for the trustee to select very safe investments which generate a minimal return as would be the case if he placed all the trust funds on deposit receipt for an extended period and did not exercise any judgment in relation to investment (*Melville v. Noble's Trs* (1896)).

The same rule applies to investments by judicial factors but in that case the judicial factor may receive authority from the court to place funds on deposit receipt if there is difficulty in finding suitable investments (*Manners v. Strong's J.F.* (1902)). In this case it was held that a judicial factor had no liability for failure to invest because he had taken the correct view that the prices at the time he could have invested were unduly high.

THE TAKING AND CONSIDERING OF ADVICE FOR INVESTMENTS

To determine whether there is sufficient diversification or whether the investments proposed are suitable or when the investments are periodically reappraised the trustee is obliged to take and consider "proper advice" (1961 Act, ss. 6(2) and (3)). This restates the common law obligation of a prudent trustee. In many cases trustees undertake an annual reappraisal of investments but volatile markets may require a more frequent cycle of reappraisals.

The words "taking and considering" are important. Not only does it imply that a sole trustee cannot take advice from himself even if he is suitably qualified to give it, but also it means that any trustee cannot instruct advice and simply not read it. He is obliged to consider any advice he instructs and cannot blindly follow the advice of financial advisers since this would amount to unlawful delegation of the trustee's responsibility.

Failure to take and consider advice may amount to a breach of trust as is exemplified in *Martin v. City of Edinburgh D.C.* (1988). The Edinburgh District Council were trustees in respect of several trusts and took a policy decision to sell all trust funds invested in South Africa. They took advice on how this could be implemented but not on whether it should be implemented. Even though the investments had increased in value it was held that this was in breach of trust because the trustees had not taken professional advice as to whether it was in the best interests of the beneficiaries to sell the investments.

The 1961 Act, s. 6(4) looks further at the matter of proper advice and states that proper advice is the advice of a person who is reasonably believed by the trustee to be qualified by his ability in and practical experience of financial matters. This would rule out taking advice from someone the trustee has never met before or whom the trustee has just met at unlikely locations such as a pub or a bus stop. That person may be a stockbroker or a surveyor but the context of the situation probably renders it unreasonable for the trustee to believe that he is properly qualified. In the context of the purchase of shares proper advice may be the opinion of a stockbroker given in the course of his business. In the context of a property investment proper advice may be the opinion of a surveyor given in the course of his business.

The advice must be given or confirmed in writing before the trustee is taken as having discharged his duty to take and consider proper advice (1961 Act, s.6(6)).

There is one exception to the rule that advice in writing must be taken as to suitability of investments, diversification of investments and continued suitability of investments and this is where there are two or more trustees and the person giving the advice is also a trustee. In such a case the trustees are still required to consider these matters but the obtaining and considering of advice in writing is not required (1961 Act, s.6(6)).

EXTENSIONS OF THE POWER OF INVESTMENT

A trust deed may be varied to include additional powers of investment if all the beneficiaries (and potential beneficiaries) consent. This is not a practical option in relation to public trusts given the number of beneficiaries.

In terms of the Trusts (Scotland) Act 1961, s. 1 the court may grant such consent on behalf of persons who by reasons of nonage or other incapacity are incapable of assenting thereto and on behalf of unascertained and unborn beneficiaries (see pp. 76 and 77).

The decision of a bench of five judges in *Henderson, Ptr* (1981) has now confirmed that the court may approve a variation in terms of the Trusts (Scotland) Act 1961, s. 1 even though the effect of such a variation is to expand the powers of the trustees beyond those permitted under the Trustee Investments Act 1961. This overrules an earlier decision of the First Division to contrary effect in *Inglis, Ptrs* (1965).

---

9. CONFLICT OF INTEREST AND PROPER MOTIVATION

INTRODUCTION

The relationship between the trustees and the beneficiary is fiduciary in nature. This means it is grounded in good faith. A trustee is a fiduciary in that he is the party to whom the truster has entrusted the trust property and he is the party the beneficiaries must trust to implement the purposes of the trust whilst he remains in office.

As a fiduciary, a trustee must keep his personal interest separate from the interests of the trust. This has two related consequences:

(a) No fiduciary may place himself in a position where his interest and his duty may possibly conflict. This is known as the rule precluding *auctor in rem suam* (which in translation means actor in his own cause); and

(b) A fiduciary should be motivated only by those consequences which are relevant to the trust and not by those which are personal to him. Although it is arguable as to whether this is a wholly separate rule, this is known as the rule requiring proper motivation.

THE RULE PRECLUDING AUCTOR IN REM SUAM

A trustee should not place himself in a position where his personal interest and his duty to the trust may possibly conflict.

Where a trustee does breach the rule of *auctor in rem suam* the following consequences occur:

(a) the trustee will be in breach of trust;

(b) where the trustee makes any profit or derives any property from the breach of trust a constructive trust will be created over that profit or property and the beneficiaries in the original trust are the beneficiaries in that constructive trust; and

(c) any transaction in which a trustee is *auctor in rem suam* is capable of reduction and is voidable at the instance of a number of parties.

The parties who may challenge a transaction on the basis that it is in breach of the rule *auctor in rem suam* include:

(a) any beneficiary who has title and interest (*Johnston v. MacFarlane* (1987));

(b) a co-trustee (see *Cherry's Trs v. Patrick* (1911));

(c) the truster provided he has a reversionary right in the trust estate or where a title to pursue the matter is expressly reserved in the trust deed;

(d) creditors of the truster, provided the truster has a reversionary right in the trust estate; and

(e) a judicial factor appointed to the trust estate (*Henderson v. Watson* (1939)).

An obligation of accounting for trust funds is imprescriptable (Prescription and Limitation (Scotland) Act 1973, Sched. 1, para. 1(f)) as is the right of a beneficiary to trace and recover trust property or to recover the proceeds from a trustee where this has been appropriated by a trustee acting as *auctor in rem suam* (Prescription and Limitation (Scotland) Act 1973, s. 7 and

Sched. 3, para. (e)). This means that breaches of trust may be pursued by a beneficiary even after the period of long negative prescription (20 years) has elapsed. For an example in which an invalid sale of land by a trustee was reduced 70 years after the sale, see *University of Aberdeen v. Town Council of Aberdeen* (1877).

The whole purpose of the common law principle of *auctor in rem suam* is to try to prevent conflicts arising rather than to try to repair the damage after a conflict has arisen. In some particular circumstances the potential for conflict of interest is so dangerous that the common law rule has been supplemented by statutory rules to ensure that a conflict of interest does not arise at all. For example in terms of the Bankruptcy (Scotland) Act 1985, s.24(2)(a) and (c) the parties excluded from the position of permanent trustee include (a) the debtor in his own sequestration and (b) a person who holds an interest opposed to the general interests of the creditors.

PRACTICAL APPLICATIONS OF THE RULES OF CONFLICT OF INTEREST

The rules relating to the avoidance of a conflict of interest apply in various circumstances to the following effect:

(a) the trustee may not transact with the trust;
(b) the trustee cannot take a personal advantage or profit from his position as trustee; and
(c) the trustee is not entitled to remuneration.

Transactions with the trust estate
Trustees may not transact in their personal capacity with the trust estate. This extends to all sorts of direct transactions including:

(a) contracts for the supply of materials. In *Aberdeen Railway Company v. Blaikie Brothers* (1854) it was held that a contract between a railway company and one of the directors in which the director contracted to supply the company with iron rails disclosed a conflict of interest and could be set aside on the basis of the rule *auctor in rem suam*.
(b) sales of heritable property to and from the trust. For an example of the latter see *University of Aberdeen v. Town Council of Aberdeen* (1877) (discussed further at p. 56);
(c) loans of money to and from the trust; and
(d) sales of goods to and from the trust. An example is *Cherry's Trs v. Patrick* (1911). A trustee in a testamentary trust continued to supply goods to the business of the truster carried on by the trustees after the death of the truster. It was held that the profit from this series of sales of goods required to be paid back to the trust by the trustee.

In any question as to whether a transaction should be interdicted as one in which the trustee has been *auctor in rem suam* it is irrelevant that there is in fact no prejudice to the trust or that the transaction is actually beneficial to the trust. It is sufficient that there is a risk of prejudice and that the interested parties object. The question of whether there has been an actual loss to the trust will of course be material if the transaction has already been carried out as the trustee will be liable to the trust in respect of that loss.

Indirect transactions and related parties

Given that the rule of *auctor in rem suam* is intended to avoid conflicts of interest the courts will be prepared to examine situations where there is a suspicion of conflict of interest. Two situations which commonly arise are:

(a) indirect transactions by the trustee; and
(b) transactions with parties related to the trustee.

An indirect transaction may occur where a trustee transacts not with the trust but with a beneficiary who in turn has transacted with the trust in relation to the same matter. Such a series of transactions could be challenged if it appeared to be a pre-arranged scheme to evade the application of the rule of *auctor in rem suam*. For example, in *Clark v. Clark's Exx* (1989) executors concluded a contract to sell part of the heritable property of the deceased's estate to a number of third parties. The third parties then assigned their right to receive the property to one of the executors in her personal capacity. The assignation was reduced on the basis that there was a conflict of interest between the executor's duty and her personal interest. This should not be taken to mean that all transactions between the trustee and a beneficiary even in relation to trust estate will be reduced. Nevertheless in this situation the onus will rest on the trustee to show that he has acted in good faith and that the beneficiary is fully aware of the nature of the transaction and the full surrounding circumstances.

The rule may in some cases extend to parties or legal entities which are closely associated with the trustee but the application of the rule to render a transaction invalid will depend on whether that party or entity acts independently causing no prejudice to the trust. This may be illustrated by two contrasting cases:

(a) In *Burrell v. Burrell's Trs* (1915) it was held that the purchase of shipping shares belonging to a trust estate by the wife of one of the trustees, on her own initiative, out of her separate estate and for an adequate consideration was valid.
(b) A partnership is recognised in Scots law as having a *persona* distinct from its constituent partners. Nevertheless where a trustee is a partner in a partnership which carries out work for the trust and is paid fees for doing so the trustee will be obliged to hold the proportion of those fees to which he is entitled under the partnership agreement on a constructive trust for the beneficiaries (see *Henderson v. Watson* (1939)).

Obtaining of personal advantage

A trustee must not use his position as trustee to obtain any personal advantage or profit.

Where a trustee uses his position to obtain property for himself the trustee becomes a constructive trustee of any property that he obtains as a result of the breach of trust and any profit or advantage that he derives from the breach. A good example is the case of *University of Aberdeen v. Town Council of Aberdeen* (1877). The Town Council of Aberdeen acted as trustees in a trust for the benefit of the professors of the University of Aberdeen. The trust property consisted of the lands of Torry. The Town Council wanted the lands for themselves and sold them secretly at an auction to themselves. They then obtained a lease from the Crown Estate of the salmon fishings *ex adverso* the lands of Torry. The salmon fishings were sub-let by the Council and a rent was received. When the University found out about the sale 80 years later they brought an action against the Town Council for breach of trust. It was held that a breach of trust had occurred and the Council were obliged to return not only the lands of Torry but also the income from the fishings. The latter is significant because at no time were the University ever owners or tenants of the fishings but the Town Council would never have been in a position to obtain a lease of these fishings if they had not abused their position as trustees.

Where a trustee has a power to exercise discretion he must not exercise it in his own favour. For example in *Inglis v. Inglis* (1983) the estate of a deceased included the tenant's interest in an agricultural lease. The executor was one of a class of people comprising the deceased's heir on intestacy. In terms of the Succession (Scotland) Act 1964 the tenant's part in the lease could be transferred to any one of these people but the executor chose to transfer the lease to himself. The transfer was reduced.

The charging of fees by trustees

The charging of fees by a trustee is prima facie a breach of the duty not to act with a conflict of interest. In the absence of contrary provision, trustees are therefore under a duty to act gratuitously. They are, however, entitled to out of pocket expenses properly incurred in connection with trust administration.

The charging of fees by a trustee may be authorised by an express clause in the trust deed (see *Lewis's Trs v. Pirie* (1912)) and also if all beneficiaries (and potential beneficiaries) consent.

In certain statutes relative to special trustees it is recognised that the trustee is entitled to remuneration. For example, when a permanent trustee distributes a debtor's estate he must first pay out the outlays and remuneration of the interim and permanent trustees (Bankruptcy (Scotland) Act 1985, s. 51(1)(a) and (b)). In terms of the Married Women's Policies of Assurance (Scotland) Act 1880, s. 2(3) it is recognised that vesting of the policy in a trustee is not prevented by a provision in the policy entitling the trustees to reasonable remuneration for professional services.

The principle will prohibit the receipt by the trustee of indirect remuneration as well as direct remuneration. Frequently where a trustee is a stockbroker, solicitor or other professional engaged in the investment business the issue may arise where the trustee places business with a particular investment house and receives a commission for doing so. This commission will not belong to the trustee personally but will be held on a constructive trust for the beneficiaries.

A difficult case arises in relation to directors' fees. In many instances the purchase of shares by a trust enables the trustees to exercise voting rights with the result that one of their number is elected to the board of directors of the company. In many other cases the holding of the shares qualifies one of the trustees to be a director without any vote. Can the trustee keep the fees which are paid to him as a director? There is little authority on the matter. In *Elliot v. Mackie & Sons* (1935) it was held that where the entitlement to be a director arose as a qualification of share ownership then the trustees could retain the director's fees and they were not held on a constructive trust for the beneficiaries. There is no Scottish authority on the second situation where trustees vote themselves into the position of directorship but, in principle, it would seem that in this case the fees would be held in a constructive trust for the beneficiaries at least where the purpose of becoming a director was to protect the interests of the trust.

CONFLICT OF INTEREST AUTHORISED BY TRUSTER

The acts of a trustee which would otherwise be invalid because of a conflict of interest may be sanctioned where the truster foresees the possibility of a conflict of interest and expressly authorises this in the trust deed. The commonest example is an express grant of a power to trustees to charge fees.

Provisions which sanction a conflict of interest are strictly construed (see *Johnston v. Macfarlane* (1987)) where a power to sell trust property to any beneficiary was held not to include a power to sell to a trustee who was also a beneficiary).

In some decisions it has been stated that a conflict of interest cannot be sanctioned by implication (*Johnston v. Macfarlane* (1987)). In other cases, however, a different view has been taken. For example, in *Coats' Trs, Ptrs* (1914) it was held that a power to sell to any beneficiary did include a power to sell to a beneficiary who was also a trustee. It may be that the two cases can be distinguished on special facts. In *Johnston v. Macfarlane* other parts of the trust deed granted rights to beneficiaries and in those parts there was an express reference to beneficiaries who were also trustees. This express statement in one part of the deed may be read as excluding an implication in another part of the deed. A more modern case has also admitted the possibility of implied sanction of a conflict of interest where the trustee is put in the position of conflict by the truster. In *Sarris v. Clark* (1995) a testator was a farmer who appointed his wife as executrix in his will. Shortly before his death he entered into contracts of co-partnery with his wife and granted a lease of the farms to the partnerships. After his death the executors entered into negotiations with the partnerships to renounce the leases and to compensate the partnerships for the renunciation. The wife was obviously on both sides of the negotiations in different capacities but it was held that this was not a breach of trust as it was the truster who had placed the wife in this position.

In one context, statutory provisions have admitted the possibility of implied sanction of a conflict of interest where a particular type of trustee is put in the position of conflict by the truster. This is where a party has died intestate and the surviving spouse's prior rights consume all of the intestate estate of the deceased. In terms of the Succession (Scotland) Act 1964, s. 9(4) it is provided that the spouse is entitled to be appointed executor. Here is a case where the right of the spouse to be both beneficiary and trustee is recognised by the general law of intestate succession to which the testator is presumed to have consented by not leaving a will.

AVOIDING THE PRINCIPLE BY OTHER MEANS

It will not avoid application of the principle of conflict of interest to show that a trustee acted with the concurrence of the other trustees. Nor may a trustee avoid the application of the principle if he retires from the meeting at which the transaction is discussed and lets his co-trustees take the decision to enter into the offending transaction.

In the absence of authority from the truster, the trustees may obtain the sanction of the consent of all the beneficiaries and potential beneficiaries to the transaction. Provided this consent is freely given and the beneficiaries are fully informed in relation to the nature of the transaction and the surrounding circumstances it will prevent the transaction from being avoided on the basis that the trustee acts as *auctor in rem suam*. For example, in *Corsar v. Mathers* (1886) a beneficiary was held not to be entitled to object to a trustee being paid for work done for the trust because the beneficiary had acquiesced in the employment of the trustee and had approved of accounts containing charges for the work. Nevertheless, the onus will fall on the trustee to show that the beneficiaries acted freely and their consent was suitably informed (*Taylor v. Hillhouse's Trs* (1901)).

Where consent cannot be obtained from the truster and all the beneficiaries the trustee probably cannot petition the court to sanction the offending transaction. The Court of Session probably has no power to authorise a transaction which would otherwise render the trustee *auctor in rem suam*. At first glance the case of *Coats' Trs, Ptrs* (1914) appears to be authority to contrary effect. In that case the trustees of a deceased party wished to sell some of the trust assets which consisted of pictures. One of the trustees who was a son of the truster wished to buy the pictures and he petitioned the court for authority to bid for the pictures at a public auction. This was a different method of sale than that authorised in the trust deed. The petition was served on all the beneficiaries but no answers to the petition were lodged by any of the beneficiaries. The petition was granted. The decision was explained in *Hall's Trs v. McArthur* (1918) as being required purely to sanction the method of sale. It was commented in *Hall's Trs* that all the beneficiaries in *Coats' Trs* had actually consented to the sale and that was the reason why the transaction was permitted despite the conflict of interest.

Whilst this does not appear to be borne out by the case report in *Coats' Trs* it does indicate that the case cannot readily be used as a precedent for the view that the court may sanction a transaction which would otherwise be voidable.

There is no rule which would generally prevent a former trustee from transacting with the trust. If a trustee is likely to be involved in a transaction where his interest as an individual may conflict with his interest as a trustee his proper course is to resign office and to transact on an equal footing with any other third party. Nevertheless the rules of conflict of interest will prevent a trustee from setting up a transaction whilst a trustee and resigning immediately before conclusion of the bargain which he then concludes as an individual. The trustee should resign in good time so that there is no suspicion of abuse of his position whilst he remained a trustee. Even in these circumstances if the transaction is challenged it may be reduced unless the trustee proves that it was not unfair to the trust.

THE REQUIREMENT OF PROPER MOTIVATION

In all his dealings with the trust a trustee must do his best to exercise a fair and rational judgment taking into account matters which are relevant to the trust only. Although it is recognised that all trustees are entitled to their own personal religious, political and moral beliefs they must not let these views influence their decisions relative to trust administration if these personal beliefs are not relevant to the trust purposes. For example, in *Martin v. City of Edinburgh D.C.* (1988) the City of Edinburgh District Council were trustees in respect of several trusts and took a policy decision to sell all trust funds invested in South Africa. They did so because of their own political antipathy to the then government in South Africa. The decision was challenged and it was held that the decision was in breach of trust as the Council had been motivated by their own values and not by the interests of the beneficiaries.

This rule would not prevent a trustee with personal beliefs which are consonant with the trust purposes from allowing those beliefs to influence his decisions relative to the trust.

Where the trustees are motivated by proper concerns this may assist in having a transaction upheld where the benefit received by the trustee is small and incidental and the principal object of the transaction is to provide some greater substantial advantage to beneficiaries who are not trustees. An example of this occurred in *Flint v. Glasgow Corporation* (1966). In that case the town council decided to benefit the community of Glasgow by installing phones in the houses of councillors. The aim was to facilitate communication with councillors. The phones were to be paid for out of the common good which was a fund held in trust for the community of the burgh. The magistrates and town councillors were the trustees. This was challenged by the auditor. It was held that although a councillor might receive a small incidental advantage he was not thereby in breach of his fiduciary duty.

Even if a trustee is motivated by his own personal beliefs in a manner which would otherwise leave him in breach of the rule, the transaction may still be upheld if the truster has sanctioned the application of personal values to transactions of the nature contemplated or if all the beneficiaries have expressly consented to the transaction in the knowledge that the trustee has applied his personal beliefs and values.

---

10. LIABILITY OF TRUSTEES TO BENEFICIARIES

INTRODUCTION

Breach of trust is a concept which is capable of application to all aspects of trust administration. It includes any form of poor management or failure on the part of the trustees which hinders or frustrates the carrying out of the trust purposes.

In most cases such a failure will cause the trust estate to diminish in value (and this is usually what will cause the beneficiaries to complain) but it is possible that a breach of trust may actually lead the trust estate to increase in value. The fact that there has been an increase in the value of the trust estate is, by itself, no defence to an action for breach of trust — although it may reduce the amount which the trustees may require to pay if they are ultimately found liable. The determining factor in deciding whether or not there has been a breach of trust is not purely financial gain or loss: the aim of a trust is the achieving of the trust purposes and not the amassing of capital.

The possible instances of breach of trust are innumerable but the following examples serve to illustrate the matter:

(a) a failure to secure trust property (see pp. 33 and 34);
(b) a failure to invest in authorised or proper investments (see pp. 50 and 51);
(c) a failure to pay the correct beneficiaries; and
(d) the making of a loan from the trust estate to one of the trustees (*Croskery v. Gilmour's Trs* (1890)).

THE DUTY OF CARE

Breach of trust arises where the trustee fails in his duty of care to the beneficiaries. The general duty of a trustee may be summarised thus. A trustee is expected to exercise due care in respect of all his actions in relation to trust property. For authority reference may be made to *Learoyd v. Whiteley* (1887).

To carry out this general duty of care it is not enough that a trustee acts to the best of his ability or in good faith. The general duty imposes an objective standard of care on trustees.

The standard of care is not the same care and diligence which a person of ordinary prudence might be expected to use in the management of his own affairs: rather it is the standard of the ordinary prudent man of business.

The standard of care required of a trustee imposes a variable level of the duty of care which imports whatever degree of care is reasonable in the circumstances. There is English authority to the effect that a higher level of care may be expected from a company which carries on business as a professional trustee than from a gratuitous trustee (see *Bartlett v. Barclays Bank Trust Co. (No. 1)* (1980)). There is as yet no authority in the form of reported cases for this view in Scotland.

To whom is the duty owed?
Liability for breach of the duties of trustee may be enforced by any of the beneficiaries or by the truster although most litigation arises in relation to the former. It cannot be enforced by a third party who is neither a beneficiary nor the truster.

If the breach of duty has been carried out by a previous trustee who has now resigned the existing trustees may enforce the liability for breach of trust against the former trustee, failing which it may be enforced by any of the beneficiaries. Where the former trustee has been granted a discharge for his acts and intromissions this will require to be reduced prior to enforcement of the liability (*Hastie's J.F. v. Morham's Exrs* (1951)).

REMEDIES FOR BREACH OF TRUST

The remedies available to a beneficiary for breach of trust include the following:

(a) interdict;
(b) damages;
(c) accounting;
(d) removal of trustees;
(e) reporting the matter to appropriate authorities for criminal prosecution or other appropriate action.

Interdict
Any beneficiary, co-trustee or truster may apply to the court for interdict against a threatened breach of trust or the continuation of a breach of trust. Where the breach has been completed and there is no indication of a repetition, interdict will not be granted.

Damages
A trustee will be liable to pay for any loss suffered by a trust as a result of his breach of trust. It is always open to a trustee to avoid having to pay by showing that the loss would have arisen even if he had carried out his duties in full (*Carruthers v. Carruthers* (1896)).

The measure of damages is the loss suffered by the trust no matter whether this is remote or not foreseeable. For example, in *Forman's Exr v. Burns* (1853) an executor failed to take steps to recover a debt of £250 until after the debtor had been sequestrated. Only £50 was eventually recovered by the trust. The executor was held liable for the shortfall of £200.

Where a breach of trust leads to benefit rather than a loss there can be no claim for damages but the trustee becomes a constructive trustee of any property that he obtains as a result of the breach of trust and any profit or advantage that he derives from the breach. The trustee is personally liable to account to the beneficiary for the profit or benefit which he obtains from the breach of trust even if he has dissipated the profit or benefit. This again arises because of the doctrine of constructive trust. A beneficiary has a right to trace trust property which has been misappropriated. Where a trustee uses trust property whether by itself or inmixed with his own property to acquire other property the property so acquired will be subject to the constructive trust and can be claimed on behalf of the beneficiaries on the trustee's insolvency (see *Jopp v. Johnston's Trs* (1904)).

A difficult situation arises where a trustee enters into a number of transactions which are in breach of trust. If one transaction leads to a profit but another leads to a loss the general rule is that the profit may not be set off against the loss. This has the result that the beneficiaries may claim the profit on the basis of the constructive trust and, in addition, pursue the trustee for the whole loss arising from the other transaction. Nevertheless, if the two transactions are in essence part of the one scheme and one could not be carried out without the other there may be room for the view that the loss and profit are to be aggregated to assess the measure of the loss from the one global transaction. There is no authority in the form of reported case law in Scotland but this approach has been followed in England (*Bartlett v. Barclays Bank Trust Co. (No. 1)* (1980)).

Accounting
Where a trustee refuses to hand over to a beneficiary the full entitlement of that beneficiary in accordance with the provisions of the trust the beneficiary may force the trustee to do so by means of an action of count, reckoning and payment. Such an action may also be used to recover the profit which a trustee has obtained as a result of a breach of trust and is held by him in a constructive trust.

An action of count, reckoning and payment has a very significant advantage over an action for damages in relation to negative prescription. The right of a beneficiary to claim trust property is imprescriptible as is exemplified in *Hobday v. Kirkpatrick's Trs* (1985). The court permitted beneficiaries to pursue trustees who had failed to pay out a sum to which they were entitled under the *mortis causa* settlement of the deceased at the appropriate date in 1973. The action was not raised until 1979, more than 6 years later but this did not preclude the raising of the action because the right to raise it was imprescriptible. The position is now governed by the Prescription and Limitation (Scotland) Act 1973 but is largely unaltered. In terms of the 1973 Act, s.7 and Sched. 3, para. (e) the trustee's liability for fraudulent breach of trust is imprescriptible. This means that it may be claimed even after the period of long negative prescription (20 years) has elapsed. By contrast, an action for damages prescribes after five years in terms of the 1973 Act, s.6.

Removal of trustees

The truster, any beneficiary or a co-trustee may petition the court for the removal from office of a trustee in respect of a breach of trust. The court has a common law power to remove a trustee from office and it will do this in cases where (a) the breach is particularly flagrant or (b) if the trustee refuses to discontinue the breach of trust.

Not all breaches of trust will merit removal from office. The matter will always be one of degree. At one end of the spectrum, small acts of mal-administration or carelessness may not justify removal but continuous neglect of trust business is likely to be sufficient. (*Macgilchrist's Trs v. Macgilchrist* (1930).) A particularly fragrant example of breach of breach of trust which will certainly lead to removal from office is where a trustee embezzles the trust funds (*Wishart & Ors, Ptrs* (1910)).

In some cases where the courts would be willing to consider removal from office, a trustee may be able to retain his position by granting an undertaking to the court that he will not repeat the breach. These cases are likely to be restricted to instances of breach of trust at the milder end of the scale such as refusal to cooperate with other trustees in relation to administrative matters (see *Dick & Ors, Ptrs* (1899)). It is highly unlikely that the court will not remove a trustee who has embezzled trust funds even if he promises never to do it again.

In certain special cases beneficiaries may have a statutory right to apply to the court to have a trustee removed from office "on cause shown". For example, in terms of the Bankruptcy (Scotland) Act 1985, s. 29 a person representing not less than one quarter in value of the creditors may apply to the sheriff for removal of the permanent trustee.

REPORTING MATTER TO THE APPROPRIATE AUTHORITIES

In many cases where a breach of trust is believed to have occurred a beneficiary, truster or co-trustee may find it cheaper, speedier and easier to avail himself of a number of remedies and rights which are available to all members of the public:

(a) If the breach of trust of the trustee amounts to a crime, such as fraud, it is always possible to report the matter to the police. A police investigation may lead to prosecution.

(b) If the breach of trust involves insider dealing in relation to securities (shares etc.) it may constitute a criminal offence in terms of the Criminal Justice Act 1993, Pt V, s. 52. In such a case the beneficiary may wish to contact the Department of Trade and Industry or the Stock Exchange with a view to prosecution. Prosecutions in Scotland may be undertaken by the Lord Advocate. For further details see MacNeil and Wotherspoon, *Business Investigations*, (Jordans 1998), chap. 4.

(c) If the trust is a Scottish public trust which has been awarded charitable status for tax purposes in terms of the Law Reform (Miscellaneous Provisions) (Scotland) Act 1990, Pt 1 any member of the public may make representations to the Lord Advocate, through the Director, Scottish Charities Office, if he or she believes there has been misconduct or mismanagement in the running of a charity or believes the charity's assets or property may be at risk. If there are grounds for concern the Scottish Charities Office may take the matter up with those responsible for the conduct of the charity's affairs — usually the trustees.

(d) In special cases statute may impose a requirement on a trustee to be a member of a certain professional body or to have particular qualifications. For example, in terms of the Bankruptcy (Scotland) Act 1985, s.24(2) a permanent trustee is required to be qualified to acts as an "insolvency practitioner". This term is defined in the Insolvency Act 1986, s. 390. As such the permanent trustee is likely to belong to one of a number of professional bodies such as the Institute of Chartered Accountants. Any interested party may write to such a body requesting investigation as to whether the acts of the trustee are worthy of scrutiny by them. If the professional body's own enquiries do uncover something unacceptable this may, in appropriate cases, lead to the trustees' expulsion from that body or even to criminal proceedings.

BREACH OF DUTY AND DEFENCES AVAILABLE TO TRUSTEES

The defences available to a trustee who breaches his duty of care and carries out a breach of trust are found in:

(a) the terms of the trust deed itself;
(b) various statutory provisions.

IMMUNITY CLAUSES IN THE TRUST DEED

The trust deed may have expressly sanctioned the breach or contain an immunity or indemnity clause absolving the trustee from the usual consequences of breach. Such clauses are construed strictly and will not absolve a trustee from conduct which is in bad faith.

A difficulty arises in relation to situations where the conduct of the trustee is careless. How careless can the trustee be without stepping outwith the protection of the immunity clause? There is some authority to the effect that immunity clauses may exempt a trustee from *mere* negligence but not *gross* negligence. The difficulty here is that in other fields, such as the law of delict, the concept of *gross* negligence has been abandoned (see *Hunter v. Hanley* (1955) although in that case two of the judges, Lord President Clyde and Lord Russell both indicated that the concept was still of use in relation to the law of trusts). Presumably *gross* negligence is something much worse than *mere* negligence but the matter remains unclear. The concept has been recently applied in *Lutea Trustees Ltd v. Orbis Trs Guernsey Ltd* (1997) where it was held that the granting of a loan by trustees without adequate enquiry or security could amount to gross negligence which was not excused by an immunity clause in the trust deed.

Statutory defences and limitations of liability

There are various statutory defences each of which relates to different matters as follows:

(a) Trusts (Scotland) Act 1921, s. 3(d);
(b) Trusts (Scotland) Act 1921, s. 30;
(c) Trusts (Scotland) Act 1921, s. 31; and
(d) Trusts (Scotland) Act 1921, s. 32.

Trusts (Scotland) Act 1921, s. 3(d)

Unless the contrary is expressed all trusts are held to include a provision that each trustee is to be liable only for his own acts and intromissions and is not to be liable for the acts and intromissions of co-trustees or for omissions. It would be very unusual for a trust deed to provide to the contrary as it would be extremely difficult to attract any party to accept the office of trustee.

This is merely declaratory of the common law and adds no greater statutory protection.

Under this subsection trustees have been held not to be liable for the acts and intromissions of their predecessors (*Mackenzie's Exr v. Thomson's Trs* (1965)).

The subsection does not prevent a trustee being liable for the breaches of trust of his fellow trustees if he himself commits a breach of his own duty to the trust. Thus, in a situation where a trustee abrogates all responsibility and does not supervise the acts of his fellow trustees, if the fellow trustees carry out a breach of trust, the first trustee may be liable for failure not to supervise.

Where more than one trustee is in breach of duty to the trust, all the trustees in breach are jointly and severally liable for the whole loss caused to the trust. A beneficiary may sue all or any one of them for the whole sum due. Unless the trust deed provides otherwise, the proportion of fault *inter se* is irrelevant and any trustee who properly pays off the beneficiary is entitled to an equal contribution from all other trustees who are liable.

The provision that a trustee will not be liable for omissions causes some difficulty in application because almost all breaches of trust may be regarded as omissions of one sort or another. For example, where a trustee fails to invest properly, this is an omission, but he may be liable for this despite the terms of the 1921 Act, s. 3(d). It seems to be the case that s. 3(d) of the 1921 Act will absolve a trustee only where there is no positive duty to act and will not remove liability where there is a clear duty to act.

Trusts (Scotland) Act 1921, s. 30

In terms of the 1921 Act, s. 30 a trustee is not to be chargeable with breach of trust for lending money on the security of any property by reason only of the proportion of the amount of the loan to the value of the property in special circumstances.

The special circumstances are if the trustee relied upon a valuation report prepared by someone the trustee reasonably believed to be a practical valuator and the amount of the loan when taken together with prior ranking loans or *pari passu* ranking loans secured on the property does not exceed two third of the valuation stated in the report.

As a matter of practicality, this means that where a trustee is to lend money on the security of heritable property he should always obtain a valuation survey from a professional firm of surveyors.

Trusts (Scotland) Act 1921, s. 31

In terms of the 1921 Act, s. 31 where a trustee commits a breach at the instigation or request or with the consent in writing of a beneficiary the court may make such order as is just to make available the interest of the beneficiary in the trust as an indemnity to the trustee or the person claiming through him.

This statute does not confer on the trustee a right of personal action against the beneficiary but allows the court to authorise the trustees not to pay that beneficiary his full entitlement. This is of limited comfort to the trustee. If the trustee is liable for more than the instigating beneficiary's interest, he must suffer the excess loss himself.

For relief to be granted to the trustee it must be shown that the beneficiary not only understood the nature of the act he was requesting but also that the performance of the act would amount to breach of trust. For example, see *Henderson v. Henderson's Trs* (1900) where it was held that a request by a beneficiary that the trust should invest in Canada did not amount to a request to invest in an imprudent way in Canada. Hence when trustees invested in a Canadian lumber company which failed they were not entitled to indemnity out of the share of the beneficiary. The beneficiary was entitled to assume that the trustees would check that it was within their power to make the specific investment.

The provision does not give the trustee absolute right to indemnity. This is given only if the court thinks fit to grant it.

Trusts (Scotland) Act 1921, s. 32

In terms of the 1921 Act, s.32 the court may relieve a trustee from liability if he acted honestly and reasonably and it appears to the court that he ought fairly to be excused for the breach of trust.

The relief granted by the court may be total or partial.

The trustee must establish both honesty and reasonableness to be granted relief. If the trustee acts honestly but not reasonably relief will not be granted (see *Clarke v. Clarke's Trs* (1925)). A trustee honestly left a sum of money on deposit receipt for two years instead of investing part of it in an annuity as the trust deed required. It was held that this was not a reasonable course of action since the result was that the annuity would be charged on the whole trust fund and not only on the part that ought to have been invested. Relief under the 1921 Act, s. 32 was refused.

The reference to fairness in the statute appears to indicate that there is an ultimate discretion on the part of the court and the trustee is not absolutely entitled to relief even if he acted reasonably and honestly. Having said that, in the vast majority of cases where a trustee has acted reasonably and honestly it will also be fair to excuse him.

A common instance of the application of the 1921 Act, s.32 is where the trust deed is ambiguous and the trustees adopt one reasonable interpretation which upon later scrutiny is declared to be inaccurate.

There is no authority in the form of reported case law in Scotland for the proposition that relief under this section will not be afforded to non-gratuitous trustees.

---

11. TRUSTEES AND THIRD PARTIES

INTRODUCTION

Trustees may acquire real rights in various types of property and be entitled to enforce personal rights of many sorts. In all these contexts the trustees will encounter and have legal relations with third parties.

A real right is a right in relation to a thing such as an item of property which may be enforced against the whole world. The right of property (*dominium*) is the primary real right. Other real rights include the tenant's right in a lease, the dominant proprietor's right to a servitude and the creditor's right in a standard security. Where a trust is entitled to a real right in any property, heritable or moveable, the title to that property will rest with the trustees who will have a right (and a duty) to enforce the real right against the rest of the world. It is clear that where a trustee is entitled to a real right in any property he simply cannot avoid legal relations with the rest of the world.

A personal right is a right enforceable not against the rest of the world but against a person or a limited class of persons. A classic example is a contractual right in respect of which another party has a contractual obligation. Broadly speaking, only the parties to the contract have rights or obligations arising from that contract. For example, where trustees enter into a contract to purchase heritage they can enforce that contract only against the seller. Where they enter into a contract to sell heritage they can enforce that contract only against the purchaser.

REAL RIGHTS

The trustees are the owners of the trust estate. It is they rather than the beneficiaries who carry out the legal dealings with third parties in respect of that estate. For example:

(a) Trustees may raise proceedings to assert a right on behalf of the trust such as an action to have a servitude declared where its existence would benefit the trust estate (*McInroy's Trs v. Duke of Athole* (1891)).

(b) Trustees may defend proceedings to prevent heritable property owned by the trust being encroached upon by third parties. For instance, they may defend an action in which a member of the public asserts a public right of way across trust land (*Anderson v. Earl of Morton's Trs* (1859)).

(c) Where necessary to preserve the development value of trust land it will be the trustees who will raise proceedings to obtain the right to divert a servitude burdening that land (*Thomson's Trs v. Findlay* (1898)).

(d) Where a trust estate benefits from a servitude or a right of common interest the trustees may raise proceedings to prevent the enjoyment of that right being frustrated by the actions of third parties (see *Taylor's Trs v. McGavigan* (1896)).

(e) Where trust property is leased it is the trustees who raise proceedings against the tenant in respect of requiring the tenant to comply with the terms of the lease (*Swan's Trs v. The Muirkirk Iron Co.* (1850)).

(f) The trustees must bear the liabilities arising from the ownership of trust property. For instance, where real conditions are enforced it is against the trustees and not the beneficiaries. (For an example of a real obligation to form a road see *Paterson v. McEwan's Trs* (1881).) Similarly, where the trustees have title to a servitude which is burdened by conditions such as an obligation to repair a canal an action to have the obligations implemented is raised against the trustees (*Tennant v. Napier Smith's Trs* (1888)).

CONTRACTS WITH THIRD PARTIES

Where trustees enter into contracts with third parties the general rule is that they are presumed to undertake joint and several personal liability in respect of those contracts.

The presumption of personal liability may be rebutted in some circumstances where it can be proved that the third party knew that the intention was to bind only the trust estate and that the third party accepted that this was the case. The onus falls on the trustee to prove that such was the case.

Exceptional cases arise where the third party who is contracting with the trust is a solicitor to the trust or one of the trustees. Both types of individual are presumed to know the extent of the trust estate and are presumed to contract with the trust on the basis that the trustees incur no personal liability. (*Ferme, Ferme & Williamson v. Stephenson's Trs* (1905)).

EXPRESS LIMITATION OF LIABILITY

The personal liability of trustees may be excluded, varied or limited by means of express provision in any contract (*Cullen v. Baillie* (1846)). Such an exclusion should be in express, unambiguous terms. It will not be readily implied from loose wording. Even where an obligation is undertaken "as trustee" this may be insufficient to avoid personal liability because the term may be regarded as merely descriptive of the identity of the party undertaking the obligation and not as a limitation of that liability (*Brown v. Sutherland* (1875)).

In the context of the conveyance of heritable property an express limitation of the trustee's liability is commonly accepted. In the disposition to the disponee the trustees usually grant warrandice from their own facts and deeds only and bind the trust estate in absolute warrandice. This means that whilst the trustees issue a warranty on behalf of the trust estate to the effect that the title to the land conveyed is absolutely good and free from defect the trustees will be liable only if a defect is found which has arisen because of something which they did. The trust estate will be liable for defects which have been caused by the actions of third parties but there will be no right to sue the trustees for these defects.

Where a contract is not in writing there will obviously be no written exclusion of personal liability on the part of the trustee. Evidence may be led from surrounding circumstances of the common intention on the part of the trustee and the third party not to hold the trustee personally liable but it may be difficult to overcome the burden of proof.

PARTNERSHIP AGREEMENTS

Where a trustee enters into a partnership he may limit his liability in a question with the co-partners by inserting a clause to that effect in the partnership agreement but he cannot restrict his liability to third parties by doing this (*Muir v. City of Glasgow Bank* (1879)). The reason for this is that the co-partner is a party to the contract of partnership and may choose to contract on a basis of limited liability of a trustee but third parties may not be aware of the contents of the partnership agreement and are not bound by it.

Where testamentary trustees entered into a deed of co-partnery with another party they were held to constitute one partner and the argument that each trustee was a separate partner was rejected (*Beveridge v. Beveridge* (1872)).

It remains open for a partnership to contract with third parties on the basis that one of the members of the firm will be liable only up to a certain financial limit. Where the relevant member of the firm is a trustee this will be one method of ensuring a limit on the liability of the trustee. Such an arrangement will be effective only on a transaction-by-transaction basis and in relation to the particular obligations contained within the relevant contract. It may be difficult to persuade third parties to contract with the partnership on that basis.

Where a trustee enters into a partnership he may limit his liability in a question with third parties by ensuring that the partnership is a limited partnership formed and registered in terms of the Limited Partnerships Act 1907. This form of partnership is infrequently encountered except in relation to agricultural tenancies where it is used as a means of avoiding security of tenure consistent with a desire to avoid exposure of the landlord to the full extent of the tenant's liabilities.

COMPANY SHAREHOLDINGS

English companies incorporated under the Companies Acts will refuse to register shares in the name of parties "as trustees". Scottish companies, in contrast, will permit the registration of share ownership in the name of parties "as trustees".

In either case the trustees may find themselves personally liable to pay the uncalled portion of the company's share capital. This is a consequence of company law rather than trust law. A limitation on the liability of certain shareholders to the extent of the trust estate would be to create an unauthorised class of shares.

If trustees do not wish to incur liability they should merely intimate their title to the company so that they are not entered on the register of members and they will be allowed a reasonable time within which to dispose of the shareholding.

TRUSTEE'S INDEMNITY

Where a trustee has had to pay any sum out of his own pocket to discharge a liability properly undertaken on behalf of the trust he is entitled to an indemnity from the trust estate.

Where a trustee properly incurs such personal liability he may proceed to pay the liability out of trust funds first without the necessity of paying the sum out of his own pocket.

The issue frequently arises in relation to expenses incurred in relation to litigation and disputes as to whether litigation was properly initiated or defended by the trustees. If trustees enter into a litigation on counsel's advice that is normally enough to entitle them to their expenses (*Buckley v. Kirk* (1908)). Trustees will not be denied reimbursement of their expenses merely because litigation is lost or because they were wrong in law provided they acted in good faith and there was a fair question for discussion.

BREACH OF TRUST — LIABILITY TO THIRD PARTIES

Where they enter into contracts with third parties the personal liability of a trustee to those third parties extends to both the liability to fulfil the obligations in the contracts and liability to pay for any breach thereof. Trustees may be liable to third parties even where the failure to perform the contract or the breach of contract is a direct result of the actions of the beneficiaries.

Where a trustee enters into a transaction, such as a contract, in breach of trust the beneficiaries may interdict the performance of the transaction prior to settlement or, in some cases, reduce the transaction after settlement. In such a situation the trustee may be liable to the trust for breach of trust and, in addition, he may remain liable to the third party for failure to properly perform the terms of the contract.

RIGHTS OF BONA FIDE THIRD PARTY ACQUIRERS

One category of acquirer in breach of trust can defeat the rights of the beneficiaries. This is the bona fide onerous transferee without notice of the trust. This generally means that, if a person in good faith acquires a property from trustees for full value without notice of the trust, this will defeat the rights of the beneficiaries to recover the property from the acquirer. This rule about acquisitions by bona fide third parties is common law recognised at and is exemplified in cases such as *Thomson v. Clydesdale Bank* (1893).

The common law rule has been supplemented by three statutory provisions which are particularly important in relation to conveyancing of heritable property:

(a) Trusts (Scotland) Act 1961, s. 2. This makes it unnecessary for a person carrying out certain dealings with trustees to inquire whether the transaction comes within the implied powers given to trustees by the first six paragraphs of the Trusts (Scotland) Act 1921, s. 4(1). These transactions are the sale, feu or lease of trust property, the borrowing of money on the security of trust estate, the excambion (swap) of any part of the trust estate, and the purchase of a suitable home for any of the beneficiaries. Other transactions are not covered by the statutory protection.

(b) Trusts (Scotland) Act 1921, s. 7. Where a deed purports to be granted by a body of trustees but is in fact granted only by a quorum, the deed is not void and its validity cannot be challenged on the ground that there has been some procedural irregularity. Such an irregularity might occur where one trustee was not consulted about a particular sale of trust property. Unfortunately the statute is not well drafted and it is not entirely clear what is denoted by the expression "a body of trustees". It could mean either the whole trustees or a lesser number who have authority to bind the trust. The former interpretation is more likely and is usually adopted by conveyancers if only for caution's sake.

(c) Succession (Scotland) Act 1964, s. 17. This protects a person who in good faith and for value has acquired title to any interest in or security over property directly or indirectly from an executor or a person deriving title from the executor. The protection is limited to challenges made on the ground that the executor's confirmation was reducible or has already been reduced or that the executor should not have transferred title to the person from whom the third party, acting in good faith and for value, has obtained title.

The common law or statutory rules concerning the bona fide acquirer do not remove the rights of the beneficiary to seek a remedy against the trustees (see Trusts (Scotland) Act 1961, s. 2(2)). A petition under the Trusts (Scotland) Act 1961, s. 5 may still be necessary to determine whether the trustees have the power to enter into the transaction but the purpose of such a petition will be to obtain the protection of the court for the trustees rather than to protect the third party acquirer.

Where the provisions of the Trusts (Scotland) Act 1961, s. 2 or the Succession (Scotland) Act 1964, s. 17 apply and a Land Certificate is issued in favour of the third party purchaser the beneficiary has no entitlement to indemnity from the Keeper of the Land Register of Scotland (Land Registration (Scotland) Act 1979, s. 12(3)(j)).

---

12. ADMINISTRATION AND SUPERVISION OF CHARITABLE TRUSTS

INTRODUCTION

The rules for the administration of Scottish public trusts which have been awarded charitable status for tax purposes are contained in the Law Reform (Miscellaneous Provisions) (Scotland) Act 1990, Pt 1 ("1990 Act"). The rules in this statute do not apply to other public trusts which are not recognised bodies even if their purpose is charitable.

Such trusts which are awarded charitable status are known as "recognised bodies". This means that the Commissioners of the Inland Revenue have given intimation that exemption from tax will be due in respect of the income of the body that is applied exclusively for charitable purposes (Income and Corporation Taxes Act 1988, s. 505).

The broad structure of the special rules for administration applying to all "recognised bodies" is as follows. The Act imposes duties on all those "concerned in the management or control" of any recognised body. This will include the trustees but may also extend to employees and in some cases to professional advisers of the trust. For simplicity's sake it is convenient to refer to this wider class of persons as "the managers" of the trust.

The structure of the 1990 Act may be further subdivided into:

(a) accounting duties;
(b) supervision; and
(c) disqualification from management.

ACCOUNTING DUTIES

The managers of the trust have a duty to keep accounts sufficient to show the transactions of the trust and its financial position (1990 Act, s. 4).

Each financial year there must be prepared a balance sheet, an income and expenditure account and report of the activities of the trust (1990 Act, s. 5).

The accounts must be preserved for six years (1990 Act, s. 4(3)) and must be available to any member of the public upon the payment of a reasonable charge in respect of the copying and postage or to the Lord Advocate free of charge (1990 Act, ss. 5(6) and 5(7)).

If the accounts are not prepared timeously or in suitable form the Lord Advocate has power to appoint a suitable person to prepare them. That person has statutory powers sufficient to enable the preparation of the accounts and his expenses will be borne jointly and severally by the managers personally (1990 Act, s. 5(10)).

SUPERVISION

The 1990 Act confers powers of supervision of recognised bodies on both the Lord Advocate and the Court of Session but the powers afforded to each differ.

The Lord Advocate has an investigative function which enables him to deal with maladministration in the past, present or future. He has the power to suspend any manager for up to 28 days if it appears to him that there is or has been misconduct or mismanagement in the administration of the trust or that it is necessary or desirable to act to protect the trust property or to secure a proper application of the trust property to the trust purposes.

The Court of Session has no investigative function which it may carry out *ex proprio motu* (on its own initiative). Instead, the powers of the Court of Session are exercisable only on the application of the Lord Advocate.

The supervisory powers of the court
The powers of the court differ according to a number of different situations:

(1) In terms of the 1990 Act, s. 7(1) the court has certain powers if it appears that there is or has been maladministration *or* there is likely to be future maladministration. If *either* of these is established the court may:
  (a) interdict *ad interim* the body from representing itself, or holding itself out, as a charity or, on the application of the Lord Advocate, from any such action as the court thinks fit;
  (b) suspend any manager;
  (c) appoint *ad interim* a judicial factor to manage the affairs of the trust;
  (d) order any person (including a bank) not to part with the trust property without the court's approval;
  (e) make an order restricting the transactions which the trust can enter into without the court's approval; and
  (f) appoint a trustee as if under the Trusts (Scotland) Act 1921, s. 22.
(2) In terms of the 1990 Act, s. 7(2) the court has certain powers if it appears to the court that there is or has been maladministration *and* there is likely to be future maladministration. If *both* of these are established the court may:
  (a) interdict the body from representing itself, or holding itself out, as a charity or, on the application of the Lord Advocate, from any such action as the court thinks fit;
  (b) remove any person concerned in the management or control of the trust;

(c) appoint a judicial factor to manage the affairs of the trust; (There were two judicial factors appointed in such circumstances in 1997–1998 see Crown Office and Procurator Fiscal Service *Annual Report 1997–1998*, p. 26); and

(d) appoint a trustee as if under the Trusts (Scotland) Act 1921, s. 22.

(3) In terms of the 1990 Act, s. 7(5) the court has a final power if it appears to it that there is or has been maladministration *and* there is likely to be future maladministration *and* it is not practicable nor in the best interests of the trust to retain its existing administrative structure *and* in the court's opinion the trust purposes would be better achieved by transferring its assets to another body. If all of these are established the court may approve a scheme presented by the Lord Advocate for the transfer of any assets of the trust to such other recognised body as the Lord Advocate specifies.

(4) In terms of the 1990 Act, s. 7(3) and (5) the court may exercise any of the powers mentioned in the three foregoing paragraphs on the application of the Lord Advocate if it is satisfied that a non-recognised body is representing itself or holding itself out as a charity and is established under the law of Scotland or is managed or controlled wholly or mainly in Scotland or has moveable or immoveable property situated in Scotland.

DISQUALIFICATION FROM MANAGEMENT

In terms of the 1990 Act, s. 8 certain persons are disqualified from being concerned with the management or control of recognised bodies. This has the effect that these persons are disqualified from trusteeship of a charitable trust.

The persons disqualified are:

(a) anyone convicted of an offence of dishonesty unless the conviction is spent under the Rehabilitation of Offenders Act 1974;

(b) any undischarged bankrupt;

(c) anyone who has been removed from office as a trustee under the 1990 Act, s. 6; and

(d) anyone subject to a disqualification order under the Company Directors Disqualification Act 1986.

In terms of the 1990 Act, s. 8(2)(b) the Lord Advocate may waive these disqualifications provided this would not prejudice the operation of the Company Directors Disqualification Act 1986.

If a disqualified person does any act of management he will be guilty of an offence but the act itself will not be invalid by reason only of its being carried out by a disqualified person (1990 Act, s.8(3) and (4)).

13. VARIATION OF TRUST PURPOSES

INTRODUCTION

After a trust is set up it may be desirable for various reasons to vary the original purposes. In some cases it may be necessary to do this to save the trust from becoming incapable of continuation. In others the variation is desirable merely to ensure easier functioning of the trust. In still others it is useful to vary the purposes of the trust to take fuller advantage of changed fiscal policy or to rid the trust of purposes which have become socially unacceptable since the trust was set up.

The variation of trust purposes is dealt with at common law and by statute.

COMMON LAW

At common law variation of the trust purposes cannot be done unilaterally by the truster, the trustees or the beneficiaries. Nevertheless there are three means which can be employed to avoid this limitation:

(a) The truster can reduce the necessity of requiring a variation by conferring wide powers of appointment on the trustees whereby the trustees may exercise considerable discretion in the choice of individual beneficiaries from a class identified by the truster;

(b) Any beneficiary without legal disability may assign or surrender his interest to a third party or another trust. However, at common law a beneficiary who had received an alimentary right could not renounce or assign it without the sanction of the court after the beneficiary had entered into possession thereof. This is the case even if the truster consents (see *Mains Trustees v. Main* (1917)). If the beneficiary in an alimentary right is not yet enjoying the gift he can renounce or assign the liferent; and

(c) A variation in trust purposes can be implemented if all the possible beneficiaries consent (*Earl of Lindsay v. Shaw* (1959)). In practice this limits the option of variation by obtaining consent because it will almost certainly be impossible to obtain the consent of all the beneficiaries in a public trust simply because there are too many of them. Even in relation to private trusts there were legal complications to render the obtaining of this consent difficult to obtain or ineffective. Consent was impossible to obtain where any of the possible beneficiaries lacked the capacity to grant it because of nonage or other legal incapacity. In this context the relevant age is 16 and a person over that age has capacity to consent to the variation of a trust. Unless judicial ratification, as provided for in the Age of Legal Capacity (Scotland) Act 1991, s. 4 has been obtained for a transaction or an arrangement involving a person of between 16 and 18 years of age he will be entitled, until he becomes 21 years of age, to apply to the court to have it set aside as being for him a prejudicial transaction within the meaning of that section.

For public trusts the common law provided for variation of purposes under the *cy-près* doctrine — by diverting the trust to a similar purpose to avoid the lapse of the trust when the initial purposes become impossible.

These devices were insufficient to cope with the range of circumstances in which a variation of trust purposes would be desirable and there has been considerable statutory innovation in this field.

STATUTE

Certain statutes provide for the variation of trust purposes in respect of certain limited classes of trusts. For example, educational endowments may be varied in terms of the Education (Scotland) Act 1980, Pt VI as amended by the Education (Scotland) Act 1981, s. 115 and Sched. 6.

The statutory provisions relevant to the variation of trust purposes generally are the Trusts (Scotland) Act 1921, ss. 5 and 16 and the Trusts (Scotland) Act 1961, s. 1. These statutes will be examined in turn.

Trusts (Scotland) Act 1921, ss. 5 and 16

The provisions in the 1921 Act are limited to making good particular defects in the machinery of a trust.

Since the provisions of the 1921 Act do not enable the court to innovate on the basic trust purposes, they are not suited to dealing with cases where these purposes are still workable but have been found to be unsuitable due to changed circumstances or to involve a liability to taxation which an alteration to the trust purposes would mitigate or remove. For that, reference must be made to the Trusts (Scotland) Act 1961.

Trusts (Scotland) Act 1961, s. 1

The 1961 Act, s. 1 permits the trustees or any of the beneficiaries (a term which includes potential beneficiaries — 1961 Act, s.1(6)) to petition the court to sanction a variation of the terms or purposes of the trust. The section falls into two separate parts as follows:

(a) The 1961 Act, s.1(1) provides for the court's approval of an arrangement varying or revoking all or any of the trust purposes or for altering the powers of the trustees in relation to managing or administering the trust estate; and
(b) Section 1(4) provides for the court's authorisation of any arrangement varying or revoking any trust purposes that entitles any of the beneficiaries to an alimentary liferent of or an alimentary income from the trust estate or any part thereof.

In summary, the 1961 Act does go further than the 1921 Act and removes two of the common law difficulties previously identified relating to consents from parties who are limited in their capacity due to non-age, etc., and renunciation of alimentary liferents.

The powers of the court under the 1961 Act are so wide that they virtually permit the court to sanction a complete resettlement.

Approval by the court — 1961 Act, s. 1(1)

The1961 Act, s.1(1) enables the court to approve an arrangement for the variation of trust purposes on behalf of persons who by reason of nonage or other incapacity are incapable of assenting thereto and on behalf of unascertained and unborn beneficiaries. The effect of the granting of these consents is that the variation is binding on all parties, including the trustees, in the same way as it would have been had all the beneficiaries for whom consent is given been alive, ascertained, *sui juris* (capable of acting for themselves), and agreed to the variation.

In terms of the 1961 Act, s. 1(1) the court cannot approve an arrangement on behalf of persons who can consent to it on their own behalf but simply have not done so or refuse to do so. If any of the beneficiaries are capable of giving their consent, it must be obtained from them before the variation can take effect.

It does not in any way lessen the difficulty of obtaining the consents of members of the public in public trusts. As a result, the 1961 Act, s. 1 as a matter of practicality cannot be used to sanction the variation of the purposes of public trusts although there is no express exclusion of such trusts in the text of the section.

The applicant cannot demand that the court approve the variation proposed in terms of the 1961 Act, s. 1(1). The wording of the statute is that "the court may if it thinks fit" approve the variation which leaves the approval in the discretion of the court. Nevertheless this discretion is constrained by the proviso to the 1961 Act, s. 1(1) which confirms that the court shall not approve an arrangement on behalf of a beneficiary if it is prejudicial to that beneficiary. In this context "prejudice" will usually be financial. In *Pollok-Morris & Ors, Ptrs* (1969) a proposed variation envisaged that the number of beneficiaries in a trust be increased to include the truster's adopted children who were not originally included. The petition sought the consent of existing beneficiaries who were still minors. The petition was not approved on the basis that the increase in the number of beneficiaries might decrease the size of the funds paid to the existing beneficiaries.

Authorisation by the court — 1961 Act, s. 1(4)

The 1961 Act, s. 1(4) enables the court to authorise the variation or revocation of an alimentary provision.

The court's decree is sufficient authority for the trustees to apply the trust funds to the new trust purposes insofar as they supersede the original alimentary provisions. Nevertheless, the variation will usually affect the interests of other persons and these parties must also consent to the variation of their right or have it provided in terms of the 1961 Act, s.1(1).

There are two conditions that must be satisfied before the court will grant authority to a variation under the 1961 Act, s. 1(4):

(a) The court must consider that the proposed arrangement must be "reasonable". This is a wider test than the "prejudicial" test under the 1961 Act, s. 1(1) and in some cases a variation may be prejudicial to the liferenter but still reasonable. In deciding what is reasonable the court must take into account all the liferenter's sources of income and such other factors as it may think material. This allows the court to take into account the effect of the variation on the fiars and this has been done in several cases particularly those in which the variation is sought for tax reasons (see *Colville, Ptr* (1962)); and

(b) The consent of the liferenter to the variation must be obtained in terms of the 1961 Act, s. 1(4) and, in practice, the court will, in addition, insist on the consents of the fiars being obtained if they are of full age and not legally disabled. If the fiars are not of full age or if they are legally disabled the court will insist upon its consent being obtained in terms of the 1961 Act, s.1(1).

PUBLIC TRUSTS AND THE CY-PRÈS DOCTRINE

The *cy-près* doctrine is a common law doctrine which applies only to public trusts. It does not apply to private trusts. Using this doctrine the courts may avoid the lapse of a public trust, when the initial purposes become impossible, by diverting the trust to a similar purpose. Unlike English law the doctrine is not restricted to charitable trusts (*Anderson's Trs v. Scott* (1914)).

Unlike variation of private trusts, a public trust cannot be varied under the *cy-près* doctrine just because the trustees wish to do this. The original purpose of the trust must have become impossible or particularly inappropriate in order to justify the application of the doctrine and only then will it be applied in the discretion of the court.

The situations in which a *cy-près* scheme may be appropriate are very varied. Examples include:

(a) A trust may have been set up to benefit a particular public institution (such as a church or hospital) which has closed down either before or after the trust was set up. In this case the court may authorise the trust funds to be paid to another similar institution.

(b) A trust may specify particular public trust purposes but fail to specify how these purposes are to be effected. In this case the court may sanction the appropriate administrative machinery.

(c) A trust may specify appropriate public purposes and machinery but have insufficient funds. In such a case the court may sanction the use of the funds for a similar, but less ambitious, purpose;

(d) In other cases where the trust has insufficient funds to achieve its purposes the court may sanction the termination of the existing trust, with the transfer of the funds to another viable trust or public body with similar purposes; and

(e) The trust may be set up to provide benefits for the victims of a particular disaster and receive funds far in excess of what is needed to achieve this. The court may provide for the excess to be diverted to another similar public purpose.

Only the Inner House of the Court of Session, acting through its *nobile officium*, may sanction a *cy-près* scheme. Although a question of *cy-près* may be raised in the Outer House (as it may be in an action of multiplepoinding) the matter must always be referred for determination to the Inner House (Trusts (Scotland) Act 1921, s. 26).

Circumstances where cy-près inapplicable

A *cy-près* scheme will be inappropriate if the truster has provided in the trust deed what is to occur to the trust funds if they require to be diverted because the trust cannot be continued. This is generally known as a trust deed with a destination-over.

A *cy-près* scheme cannot be utilised to validate *ex post facto* any acts of the trustees which are or may be *ultra vires*.

A *cy-près* scheme cannot remedy the situation where the truster has failed to set out any valid trust purposes because the purposes stated are void because of uncertainty or illegality.

A *cy-près* scheme is not available where the original purposes of the truster are so singular and unique that no similar replacement purposes can be found.

Impossibility

For the *cy-près* to apply there must be a failure of the public trust purposes. This means that it must have been impossible to carry out the purposes or, at least, wholly inappropriate to carry them out in their existing form.

A series of cases has indicated that trust purposes do not become impossible simply because of difficulty in carrying them out, shortage of trust funds or a shortage of qualified beneficiaries. To this extent the variation of public trusts under the *cy pres* doctrine is very different from the variation of private trusts. For example, in *Scotstown Moor Children's Camp Trs, Ptrs* (1948) the object of a charitable organisation was to run a summer camp for needy and ailing children. During the Second World War the running of the camp was suspended and the rationing of food made it difficult to run the camp again. A petition was presented to the court to use the *cy-près* doctrine to transfer the trust assets to the local Boys' Brigade battalion. The petition was refused on the basis that the objects of the original charity had not failed and its methods had not become impracticable.

In contrast to this strict approach there are some other cases which indicate that a more liberal approach will be taken and the courts have accepted that it is not necessary to show absolute impossibility. For example, in *Glasgow YMCA Trs, Ptrs* (1934) a voluntary association had a large capital fund but a deficit in their income. The court approved a variation to allow them to apply part of the capital fund to pay off the deficit in income even although the trust could have continued to exist for a period without doing this. The court took the view that a variation was appropriate because the work of the trust would be severely hindered without a variation.

The existence of a strict approach and a liberal approach made giving advice very difficult. It was almost impossible to predict which approach the court would adopt in particular cases. The difficulty has now been elided by the enactment of a statutory power to enable the court to approve a scheme to vary public trusts under the Law Reform (Miscellaneous Provisions) (Scotland) Act 1990, ss. 9 and 10.

Initial and supervening impossibility

In applying the conditions to be satisfied before the *cy-près* doctrine is applied a distinction must be made between supervening impossibility and initial impossibility. For example, where a trust is set up to benefit a hospital and the hospital closes years after the trust is set up, that is supervening impossibility. Where the hospital shuts prior to the trust coming into effect or never existed at all that is initial impossibility.

In the case of supervening impossibility the application of the *cy-près* doctrine is clear. Because the trust has commenced the truster will have divested himself of all interest in the property and there is no room for the application of the doctrine of resulting trust if the trust purposes subsequently fail.

In the case of initial impossibility the interest of the truster will not have been effectively terminated and he retains a residual right in the property if the trust cannot take effect. In such a situation the trust property will revert to the truster as part of a resulting trust and the *cy-près* doctrine cannot be applied unless it can be demonstrated that there is an underlying general intention on the part of the truster to benefit public purposes.

A practical point which frequently arises is where a truster establishes a trust in favour of a named organisation or charity. It will not amount to impossibility if the named organisation changes its name and it may claim the benefit under the trust under its new name. A more difficult case arises where a named organisation such as a church amalgamates or splits into a number of groups. In this sort of case there is a high risk of litigation as each group may attempt to claim the benefit by means of an action of multiplepoinding. The *cy-près* doctrine may be applied as part of such an action.

General charitable intention

Where there is initial but not supervening impossibility the courts will grant a *cy-près* scheme only if the terms of the trust deed show that the truster had a general intent to benefit public purposes. This may be distinguished from a situation where the truster intends to benefit a particular institution or body which happens to have public purposes.

The distinction will require an examination of the words of the trust deed. This means that each case must be decided on its own facts and circumstances. The case law is of limited value but, nevertheless, demonstrates the fine distinction which may require to be made. Two contrasting cases serve to illustrate the point:

(a) In *Hay's J.F. v. Hay's Trs* the testatrix left a will which expressly stated that a particular mansion house was to be maintained by her trustees "either as a home for aged and infirm Shetland seamen, a surgical hospital or a convalescent hospital, whichever the said trustees may consider the most beneficial for the islands of Shetland". After the death

of the testatrix it became clear that it was impossible to open the rest home or hospital but the words used by the testatrix were wide enough to demonstrate a general intent to benefit the public. Therefore the *cy-près* doctrine could apply.
(b) By contrast, in *McRobert's Trs v. Cameron & Ors* (1961) a trust was created with the purpose of constructing and fitting out a private ward in a particular hospital. There was no reference in the trust deed to the benefit of the local community as a whole. Before construction of the ward began, the hospital was closed down. A *cy-près* scheme was applied for. It was refused on the basis that there was no general intent to benefit public purposes. The bequest was merely a gift to a particular institution which served the public and it could not be said that the truster wished another similar institution to benefit if the original gift failed.

It is sometimes stated that Scots law accepts the English law rule that a general charitable intent will be presumed where a gift is made to an institution which never existed but a presumption of intent to benefit only a specified institution will be presumed where the gift is made to a named institution which did exist at one time but has ceased to exist. For authority see the *obiter* remarks of Lord Dunedin in *Burgess's Trs v. Crawford* (1912). Although this rule has been applied in one subsequent Scottish case — *Tod's Trs v. The Sailors' and Firemen's Orphans' and Widows' Society* (1953) — the rule is somewhat illogical and may be criticised as reading far too much into the wording of the trust deed. It remains to be seen if the rule will be followed in a modern Scottish case.

Approximation
Whether the failure of the original trust purposes is initial or supervening, a *cy-près* scheme will require that the proposed replacement purposes are approximate to the original purposes. The rationale is that the new purposes must be sufficiently similar to enable the court to regard them as falling within the truster's original intentions.

The requirement of approximation is easier to fulfil where the problem with the implementation of the original trust purposes arises due to a failure of the trust machinery. The new arrangements will be acceptable if they merely remedy the administrative defects.

The requirement of approximation is more difficult to fulfil where it is the actual original purpose which is impossible. The court will only sanction a scheme which bears a reasonable resemblance to the original purposes of the trust. For example, in *Glasgow Royal Infirmary v. Mags of Glasgow* (1888) an existing public trust had as its purpose the building of a convalescent fever home. The town council established a fever hospital. The trustees petitioned the court to sanction a scheme to divide the trust funds to support two purposes: (a) the erection of nurses' homes at the Glasgow Royal Infirmary and (b) the support of a society for fever and smallpox hospitals. The court approved the scheme but only on the basis that all the funds went to the society as this was closest to the original wishes of the parties who donated funds to the original trust.

An important aspect in finding a suitable approximation is any specific limitations mentioned by the truster. Significant in this regard are any original geographical limitation on the original purposes. For example, in *Glasgow SPCA v. National Anti-Vivisection Society* (1915) the court refused to sanction a scheme which proposed the transfer of funds from a trust set up to benefit only Scottish institutions to an English society.

When a *cy-près* scheme is contemplated it is usually for the party drafting the scheme or the reporter appointed by the court to identify a suitable approximate purpose. This will not be done by the court *ex proprio motu* except where the issue arises as part of an action of multiplepoinding, in which case the Lord Ordinary will deal with the matter.

STATUTORY VARIATION OF PUBLIC TRUSTS

A statutory power to enable the court to approve a scheme to vary public trusts was introduced by the Law Reform (Miscellaneous Provisions) (Scotland) Act 1990, ss. 9 and 10. This power applies to all public trusts whether created before or after the 1990 Act came into operation.

The statutory power to vary is in addition to the *cy-près* jurisdiction of the Court of Session and the statutory grounds of variation overlap to some extent with the grounds upon which the *cy-près* jurisdiction would be exercised. There is, however, no need to prove impossibility of fulfilling trust purposes under the statute. There may be cases where a proposed variation of a trust falls outwith the scope of the statutory grounds and a *cy-près* jurisdiction is still relevant (see *The Mining Institute of Scotland Benevolent Fund Trs, Ptrs* (1994) and *Winning & Ors, Ptrs* (1999)).

The statutory powers to vary a public trust differ from the *cy-près* jurisdiction in that *cy-près* jurisdiction is restricted to the *nobile officium* of the Court of Session but the 1990 Act gives jurisdiction to both the sheriff court and the Court of Session.

The aims of the statute were to make the variation of public trusts simpler, quicker and cheaper. Consonant with this is a simplified approach to vary small public trusts (trusts with a very small annual income) in the 1990 Act, s. 10. Under this method the need for court procedure may be avoided altogether and the variation effected by resolution of the trustees rather than by court decree.

Grounds of variation

Under the 1990 Act, s. 9 the court may approve a scheme for the variation of a public trust on the application of the trustees if it is satisfied that:

(a) one of four statutory grounds has been established; and
(b) the trust purposes proposed in the new scheme will enable the resources of the trust to be applied to better effect consistently with the spirit of the trust deed, having regard to changes in social and economic conditions since the time the trust was created.

The four grounds for variation are set out in the 1990 Act, s. 9(1):

(a) that the purposes of the trust have been fulfilled so far as is possible or can no longer be given effect to; or
(b) that the purposes of the trust provide a use for only part of the trust property; or
(c) that the purposes of the trust were expressed by reference to an area which has ceased to have effect for these purposes or by reference to a class of persons or area which has ceased to be suitable or appropriate for the trust; or
(d) that the purposes of the trust have been adequately provided for by other means, or have ceased to be entitled to charitable status for revenue matters or have otherwise ceased to provide a suitable and effective method of using the trust property, having regard to the spirit of the trust deed.

The scheme approved by the court may include a transfer of assets to another public trust or the amalgamation of the trust with one or more other public trusts (1990 Act, s.9(3)).

The application for variation under the 1990 Act must be intimated to the Lord Advocate. He is entitled to enter appearance as a party to the proceedings and lead such proof and enter such pleas as he thinks fit. (1990 Act, s. 9(6)).

Variation of small public trusts
The Law Reform (Miscellaneous Provisions) (Scotland) Act 1990, s. 10 contains a simplified procedure for the variation of small public trusts. These are public trusts whose annual income does not exceed £5,000. This figure may be amended by the Secretary of State by order (1990 Act, s. 10(15)).

In such cases the trustees can do one of three things as follows:

(a) modify the trust purposes; (1990 Act, s.10(3));
(b) wind up the trust by transferring the assets to another trust the purposes of which are not dissimilar in character to those of the trust to be would up as to constitute an unreasonable departure from the spirit of the trust deed (1990 Act, s.10(8)); or
(c) amalgamate the trust with one or more trusts the purposes of which are also not dissimilar (1990 Act, s. 10(10)).

Such a variation is not effected by court petition but simply by the trustees passing a resolution that the purposes of the trust be altered or that the trust be wound up or amalgamated. The resolution may be passed whenever a majority of the trustees are of the opinion that any of the four grounds for variation have been established (1990 Act, s.10(1)). These are identical to the four grounds for variation of a large public trust by the court.

In passing the resolution the trustees have four duties as follows:

(a) they must have regard to the circumstances of the locality of the trust, if the trust purposes relate to a particular locality;

(b) they must ensure that the new purposes or the trust to which the assets are being transferred or with which the trust is being amalgamated have the same charitable status as the original provisions;

(c) they must have regard to the extent to which it may be desirable to achieve economy by amalgamating two or more charities; and

(d) they must ascertain that the trustees of the trust to which the assets are being transferred or with which the trust is being amalgamated agree to the proposed transfer or amalgamation.

The variation will be effective two months after the resolution has been properly advertised.

The procedure does not give carte-blanche to the trustees to do what they like. There are two controls, one being statutory and the other arising from common law. First, the Lord Advocate has power to intervene and prevent the modification of the trust purposes, the transfer of assets or amalgamation of the trust if it appears to him that the proposed variation should not go ahead (1990 Act, s. 10(14)). Secondly, any resolution is open to reduction at the instance of anyone having interest in appropriate cases.

---

14. TERMINATION OF TRUSTS

INTRODUCTION

Some public trusts may exist in perpetuity. These, however, are exceptional cases, and the vast majority of trusts will come to an end when the trust purposes have been implemented and all trust property distributed to the appropriate beneficiaries.

A provision which is declared to be alimentary cannot be renounced by a beneficiary once the beneficiary has started to enjoy the benefit. The trust must be continued to protect the alimentary right, even if the person who is entitled to it is also vested in the fee or all other persons interested concur in the demand for termination and even if the truster consents. The only way in which the trust may be brought to an end in these circumstances is if the variation or revocation of the trust purpose to which the alimentary right relates has been authorised by the court (Trusts (Scotland) Act 1961, s. 1(4)).

A trust may be brought to an end by various parties as follows:

(a) the truster (revocation);
(b) the creditors of the truster (reduction);
(c) the trustees;
(d) the beneficiaries.

The circumstances in which these parties may bring the trust to an end are very different and are outlined below.

TESTAMENTARY TRUSTS — REVOCATION BY THE TRUSTER

As a general rule a testamentary trust may be revoked by the testator at any time prior to his death. After his death the truster is obviously in no position to revoke such a trust.

A declaration that a testamentary deed is irrevocable is of no effect to prevent revocation prior to the testator's death because it also can be revoked by the testator. It makes no difference that the deed has been delivered to the beneficiaries prior to the testator's death so long as it is clear that it is truly testamentary in character.

A person may bind himself during his lifetime to bequeath his estate in a particular way, and if he does so, the bequest will be irrevocable in consequence of his obligation. An example of this is to be found in *Paterson v. Paterson* (1893). A mother executed a trust disposition and settlement in favour of her son in return for sums of money which he advanced to her under an agreement. She was held to have been disabled by that agreement from revoking the trust disposition and settlement and disposing of her property otherwise on her death. Although that was a case of an onerous contract, it is of no importance whether the agreement is gratuitous or onerous.

INTER VIVOS TRUSTS — REVOCATION BY THE TRUSTER

The truster retains the right to revoke an *inter vivos* trust for so long as the following apply:

(a) the property in the trust estate has not yet passed from the truster to the trustees;
(b) there are no beneficiaries in existence, or, if there are beneficiaries in existence, none has a vested interest;
(c) the truster intends the trust to be revocable.

A deed may be revocable as regards one provision and irrevocable as regards another (*Leckie v. Leckies* (1776)).

Passing of property
This matter has been generally addressed above (see p. 12) and only a number of specialities will be noted here.

Trusts created under the Married Women's Policies of Assurance (Scotland) Act 1880, s. 2 are an exception to the common law rule that delivery of the trust property to the trustees is essential to constitute an irrevocable trust. Under the 1880 Act the policy vests in the trustees immediately upon its being effected and the trust is irrevocable. There is no need to deliver either the trust deed or the trust property to the trustees.

In relation to heritable property actual delivery is not possible but recording of the deed in the Sasine Register or registration of the title in the Land Register of Scotland is regarded as the equivalent of delivery (*Bruce v. Bruce* (1675)).

In relation to shares in a limited company the registration of the name of the trustees in the register of members of the company is treated as the equivalent of delivery even if the share certificates are retained by the truster (*Lord Advocate v. Galloway* (1928)).

Existence of beneficiaries

There must be some beneficiaries in existence before an *inter vivos* trust can be held to be irrevocable.

Where the trust estate is directed to be held for persons other than the granter but such persons are not in existence or not yet ascertained, the trust is still revocable even if the deed expressly states that it is irrevocable. This has been applied in a number of reported cases. For example, in *Burn-Murdoch's Trs v. Tinney* (1937) funds had been settled by a wife under an antenuptial contract with an alimentary liferent in her own favour and the fee directed to be paid to the issue of the marriage . The marriage was dissolved without there being any issue and the wife wanted to reclaim her funds by revoking the trust. It was held that she could do this and the capital fell to be repaid to her as the whole purposes applicable to the intended marriage had been fulfilled and there were no issue who could be regarded as beneficiaries.

A trust may begin as a revocable trust and become irrevocable because of the birth of beneficiaries. In other circumstances, a trust may begin as an irrevocable trust and become revocable because of the death of all beneficiaries.

Beneficial interest of beneficiaries

A trust becomes irrevocable only after a beneficiary obtains a beneficial interest in the trust property to the effect that he may enforce the trust against the truster and the trustees. Otherwise stated, the test is whether the beneficiaries are granted a *jus quaesitum tertio.*

This test is clearly satisfied where the beneficiary takes immediately a vested interest in the trust fund. Less than this, however, will suffice to render a trust irrevocable. For example, beneficiaries in a discretionary trust may have no immediate vested interest in trust property but they have a title to enforce the trust sufficient to prevent revocation without their consent. Similarly, the vesting of a particular gift in a beneficiary may be subject to a contingency (such as the attainment of a certain age) and there can be no guarantee that this contingency will certainly occur. However, the beneficiaries still have an immediate right to enforce the trust against the truster and the trust will be immediately irrevocable on creation of the trust long before the occurrence of the contingency.

Intention of truster

In relation to *inter vivos* trusts an express declaration that the trust is revocable by the truster will receive effect except where the trust deed creates an alimentary liferent in favour of a beneficiary other than the truster and the beneficiary has entered into possession.

If the deed states that it is irrevocable the trust can be revoked by the truster only if he obtains the consent of all the beneficiaries who have obtained a beneficial interest.

If the deed of trust in relation to an *inter vivos* trust is silent as to revocability the law resorts to a presumption that the trust is revocable by the truster without the consent of the beneficiaries.

This presumption may be overcome if the powers granted to the trustees are so extensive that it is clear that the truster has relinquished all control over the trust property. A power which is given to the trustees to make advances of capital to the granter or to provide for the maintenance and education of children during the granter's lifetime favours irrevocability. The existence of such a power in the trustees does not imply a right in the granter to re-acquire the property because it is subject to the discretion of the trustees and must be exercised in accordance with the conditions of the trust. A power to require payment of a specified part of the trust funds conveyed to the trustees tends to emphasise the irrevocable character of the conveyance of the remainder of the funds (*Lawson's Tr. v. Lawson* (1938)).

The presumption is more likely to be overcome in a trust of a specific fund or item of property than a trust of the whole assets of the truster (see *Lawrence v. Lawrence's Trs* (1974)).

A trust will not be regarded as revocable simply because it is gratuitous (*Robertson v. Robertson's Trs* (1982)).

REDUCTION BY THE CREDITORS OF THE TRUSTER

Insolvency of the truster does not entitle the truster to revoke the trust nor is a trust revoked without any legal process upon the sequestration of the truster. In certain cases, however, a creditor and a permanent trustee in bankruptcy may reduce a trust deed. In such a case the trust will come to an end and the property will vest in the permanent trustee for the purposes of the sequestration.

In terms of the Bankruptcy (Scotland) Act 1985, s. 34 where a sequestrated party has made a gratuitous alienation within a period of two years prior to the sequestration, a creditor and a permanent trustee in bankruptcy may challenge the alienation. If the challenge is successful the court will reduce the alienation. In applying this the following matters are relevant:

(a) The term gratuitous alienation generally denotes a gift or transfer for insufficient consideration made at a time when the granter's liabilities exceeded his assets;

(b) The meaning of the term "alienation" is wide enough to include the granting of a deed of trust;

(c) Where the grantee in respect of the alienation is an "associate" of the granter the period of two years prior to the sequestration is extended to five years. The term "associate" is widely defined in the Bankruptcy (Scotland) Act 1985, s. 74 but generally denotes persons who are related by birth or marriage, connected by the relationship of employment or companies in the same group of companies; and

(d) The court will not grant reduction if the alienation was a reasonable gift made for charitable purposes. "Charitable" is defined as any charitable, benevolent or philanthropic purpose whether or not it is charitable within the meaning of any rule of law (Bankruptcy (Scotland) Act 1985, s. 34(4) and (5)). In theory this may render certain trust deeds relative to public trusts incapable of reduction. In practice, however, the exception is more likely to be appropriate to gifts to existing charitable trusts rather than deeds creating a new trust.

TERMINATION BY THE TRUSTEES

At common law the general rule is that the trustees may terminate a trust only by effectively and completely fulfilling the purposes of the trust. This usually occurs where the trustees distribute all trust property in accordance with the provisions of the trust deed.

In certain circumstances where the trust cannot continue to function properly the trustees may petition the court to bring an existing trust to an end as part of a *cy-près* scheme and under certain statutory provisions (see Law Reform (Miscellaneous Provisions) (Scotland) Act 1990, s. 9)).

TERMINATION BY THE BENEFICIARIES

As a general rule the beneficiaries may compel the trustees to bring the trust to an end if they all agree to this course of action. The agreement of every one of the beneficiaries is, however, essential to the operation of this principle. If any one of them is incapable of giving his consent due to non-age or other disability or is as yet unascertained or unborn the trust must be continued for his benefit. There is a power of the court to approve an arrangement for the variation of trust purposes on behalf of such persons under the Trusts (Scotland) Act (1961), s. 1(1) (see pp. 76–78).

This general rule is subject to two major exceptions:

(a) There is no such right if it would prejudice the trustees in the proper administration of the trust. The trustees may be able to resist the claim of a particular beneficiary to bring the trust to an end and grant a conveyance in his favour on the ground that they have entered into some arrangement for the benefit of the trust as a whole which cannot be terminated without loss to the other beneficiaries. For example, in *De Robeck v. Inland Revenue* (1928) the trustees had entered into an arrangement to pay estate duty in 16 half-yearly instalments. It was held that the trustees were entitled to maintain the trust until the estate duty was paid off and the trustees themselves were free from any further liability. If, however, all of the beneficiaries, including those who would suffer loss if the administrative arrangements were to be disrupted, concur in making the demand it would seem that the trustees have no right to refuse to give effect to it.

(b) Such a power on the part of beneficiaries cannot be used to renounce any alimentary provision which a beneficiary has started to enjoy. The court may, however, authorise variation of alimentary provisions under the Trusts (Scotland) Act 1961, s. 1(4).

A trust may be brought to an end by the beneficiaries where the remaining purposes of a trust are purely administrative and the beneficiary has acquired an unqualified vested right in the trust property (*Miller's Trs v. Miller*(1890)).

The case of all the beneficiaries bringing the trust to an end should be distinguished from the case of one or more beneficiaries renouncing their rights as beneficiaries. In the latter case the trust does not come to an end but continues in force in respect of the remaining beneficiaries.

DISCHARGE OF THE TRUSTEES

Before he denudes the trust estate (whether on resignation or on the passing of any trust property to a beneficiary) a trustee is entitled to a discharge provided he has carried out his functions properly and is not in breach of trust. The discharge will protect the trustee from an action raised by that beneficiary in respect of any future potential liability arising from the trust.

A trustee may refuse to denude the trust estate until he is granted a valid discharge of his own acts and intromissions. Unless the trust deed provides to the contrary, he cannot refuse to denude until he has received a discharge of the intromissions of predecessors (*Mackenzie's Exr v. Thomson's Trs* (1965)).

Each trustee is individually entitled to a discharge but it is common to find a discharge granted in favour of all existing trustees.

Methods of discharge

The trust deed may make provision for the method of discharge of the trustees. In a trust deed it is competent to confer a power to grant a discharge on parties who are not beneficiaries. This is useful where the beneficiary is *incapax* due to lack of age and the party upon whom power is conferred is the parent of the beneficiary.

In the absence of any special provision in the trust deed or statute a discharge may be obtained from any of the following:

(a) the beneficiaries;
(b) co-trustees; and
(c) the court.

A discharge obtained from the wrong person is a nullity and as worthless as a piece of waste paper (*Hastie's J.F. v. Morham's Exrs* (1951)).

Although a discharge may be implied from circumstances in appropriate cases, it is prudent to ensure that the discharge is contained in written form, preferably in a form which is subscibed by the beneficiary and, if large sums are involved, attested by a witness according to the requirements of the Requirements of Writing (Scotland) Act 1995, s. 3(1).

Discharge by the beneficiaries

A discharge granted by the beneficiaries is the usual method of a trustee's obtaining a discharge.

Where the beneficiary is merely entitled to a legacy of a specific amount the trustee is entitled only to a receipt for the payment of the appropriate sum (*Fleming v. Brown* (1861)).

A more expansive discharge comprising a receipt and a discharge of the trustee's intromissions is appropriate where the subject of the specific legacy comprises the whole of the trust estate. This will be particularly detailed where the trust is being wound up contemporaneously with the payment of the legacy.

Discharge from co-trustees
If it is not at variance with the terms or purposes of the trust, trustees have a power to discharge trustees who have resigned and the representatives of trustees who have died (Trusts (Scotland) Act 1921, s. 4(g)).

A discharge properly granted by co-trustees is as valid as one granted by the beneficiaries.

If the trustees have wrongly discharged a trustee who has resigned they may be liable to the beneficiaries for breach of trust.

Discharge by the court
The Trusts (Scotland) Act 1921, s. 18 provides that where a trustee who has resigned or where the representatives of a trustee who has died cannot obtain a discharge of his acts and intromissions from the remaining trustees and when the beneficiaries of the trust refuse or are for some reason unable to grant a discharge, the resigned trustee or the representatives of the deceased trustee may petition the court for a discharge. The court will then make such inquiry as it considers necessary and has a discretion as to whether to grant the discharge or not.

If either the trustees or the beneficiaries are available and willing to grant a discharge the court cannot intervene in terms of the Trusts (Scotland) Act 1921, s. 18.

The Trusts (Scotland) Act 1921, s. 18 may be used where there is a doubt as to whether the trustees are actually entitled to the discharge.

Effect of discharge
The effect of the discharge is to protect the trustees from any future liability under the trust and to secure their intromissions from challenge. In short, the discharge ends the trustee's liability under, and arising from, the trust.

In exceptional cases a discharge may be reduced in which case the trustees may still be held to account for their intromissions and for breach of trust. Grounds of reduction include fraud, misrepresentation and essential error. In any action for reduction the beneficiary must aver the specific facts with which he was not acquainted at the date of the discharge (*Campbell v. Montgomery* (1822)).

SPECIAL STATUTORY CASES

In terms of the Bankruptcy (Scotland) Act 1985, s. 57 provision is made for the issue of a certificate of discharge to the permanent trustee in a sequestration. Where it is appropriate to be granted, the certificate of discharge is granted by the Accountant in Bankruptcy. Should he refuse to grant the certificate of discharge, the permanent trustee may appeal to the sheriff who, if satisfied that a discharge should be granted, may ordain the Accountant in Bankruptcy to grant the certificate of discharge.

In terms of the Bankruptcy (Scotland) Act 1985, s. 57(5) the certificate of discharge has the effect of discharging the permanent trustee from all liability (other than liability arising from fraud) to all the creditors or to the debtor in respect of any act or omission of the permanent trustee in exercising the functions conferred on him in the 1985 Act.

---

15. PRIVATE INTERNATIONAL LAW

INTRODUCTION

The rules of law outlined in these notes are applicable to trusts governed by Scots law. In many cases, however, trusts have international aspects. For example, some trust property may be situated abroad and some beneficiaries may reside abroad.

A number of particular instances of such international aspects have already been mentioned:

(a) A trust of foreign land is invalid if the legal system where the land is situated does not give effect to trusts (*Brown's Trs v. Gregson* (1920)).
(b) Residence abroad is no bar to trusteeship, although by statute it is made a ground on which, in certain circumstances, the court may remove a trustee. (1921 Act, s. 23).

Apart from these two points of detail, two more general questions arise from this sort of situation:

(a) In what circumstances will a trust be governed by the law of Scotland?
(b) In what circumstances will a trust governed by a foreign legal system be recognised and thereafter given effect to in Scotland?

Both questions are answered by the Recognition of Trusts Act 1987. The Act was passed in order to allow the United Kingdom to ratify the Hague Convention on the Law Applicable to Trusts and Their Recognition. The U.K. ratified this convention in November 1989.

COMPARISON OF THE PROVISIONS OF THE 1987 ACT AND THE CONVENTION

The 1987 Act sets out the Convention in a Schedule and the 1987 Act, s. 1(1) provides that the provisions of the Convention shall have the force of law in the United Kingdom.

Despite this incorporation the extent of the application of the 1987 Act and the Hague Convention are not identical. The Convention is restricted to trusts "created voluntarily and evidenced in writing" (Art. 3) but the 1987 Act, s. 1(2) extends the application of the Convention rules in the U.K. to "any other trusts of property arising under the law of any part of the United Kingdom" and also to any other trust arising "by virtue of a judicial decision whether in the United Kingdom or elsewhere".

This means that trusts which are not created voluntarily or evidenced by writing such as constructive trusts will be covered provided they arise under the law in any part of the U.K. Trusts created judicially anywhere in the world will be covered even if the country from which that trust arises is not a signatory to the Hague Convention. Article 21 of the Convention permits states to restrict its application to contracting states but the U.K. has not done so.

WHEN IS A TRUST A SCOTTISH TRUST?

The position was previously governed by the common law and is now governed by the 1987 Act. The Articles of the Hague Convention contain the relevant rules and these are largely brought into U.K. law as a schedule to the 1987 Act. The Convention has retrospective effect and so it applies to trusts which became effective both before and after ratification of the Convention. (Art. 22 of the Convention).

Under the Hague Convention a trust can become a Scottish trust by one of two alternative methods:

(a) the express or implied choice of the truster; and
(b) where no such choice is made, the law will determine Scots law to be the legal system with which the trust has closest connection.

Express or implied choice of truster

The truster may choose Scots law by an express or implied provision to that effect in the trust deed (Art. 6). This may be classified as the subjectively chosen applicable law.

If a clause choosing Scotland as the applicable law is inserted in a trust deed, care should be taken to select the legal system of Scotland or the law of Scotland rather than the law of the United Kingdom or "British law". The United Kingdom does not have a single legal system and there is no such law as "British law".

A different legal system may be chosen for different aspects of the trust (Art. 9). It is even possible under Art. 10 to provide that the chosen law may subsequently change. This could be useful if , for example, all trust property in the originally chosen legal system is sold and new property purchased within another legal system.

Where there is no express choice of law clause a choice may be implied from the provisions of the trust deed. For example, the use of Scottish terminology such as "truster" rather than the English term "settlor" may imply that Scots law is to govern the trust as would reference in the trust deed to exclusively Scottish legislation.

Objectively determined applicable law

By Art. 7 it is provided that "where no applicable law has been chosen, a trust will be governed by the law with which it is most closely connected". Scots law will obviously apply where the connections of the trust with that legal system are strongest. This will be applied in two distinct types of cases. First, where the truster makes no express choice of law and, secondly, where the express choice of law fails for some reason for example, where the truster chooses a legal system which does not recognise trusts.

Article 7 sets out a number of features which are relevant to the determination of the legal system most closely connected with a trust but does not specify that any of them should be of any greater importance than the others. What is clear is that the test of closest connection does not amount to a mere majority of the listed features. The list, which is not exhaustive, includes the following:

(a) the place of administration of the trust chosen by the truster;
(b) the location of the assets of the trust;
(c) the place of residence or place of business of the trustees;
(d) the objects of the trust and the place where they are to be fulfilled.

As Art. 7 is not exhaustive it may be assumed that in the determination of the legal system with which a trust is most closely connected other factors of relevance which are not listed in Art. 7 may be considered. These include:

(a) the current residence of the beneficiaries;
(b) the domicile of the truster; and
(c) the terms of the trust which, by themselves, are insufficient to amount to an express or implied choice under Art. 6.

The terms of Art. 7 assume that only one legal system will have the closest connection with the trust and it is difficult to see how Art. 9 (which permits different aspects of the trust to be governed by different laws) can apply where the law of the trust is governed under Art. 7.

Matters governed by the applicable law

However the applicable law is chosen or determined that law will be the law to govern all aspects of the trust subject to the following three exceptions:

Where a second legal system is chosen to govern a particular aspect of the trust that second legal system will deal with that particular aspect (Art. 9).

The applicable law will deal with all trust issues once the trust is established but will not deal with issues before the trust is established such as capacity of the truster and delivery of the trust deed (Art. 4). These will be dealt with by the legal system chosen through the forum's pre-existing conflict of law rules relative to these issues.

Taxation matters are excluded in terms of Art. 19. A truster cannot avoid the application of U.K. tax legislation by a choice of law clause. Nor can a foreign truster obtain British tax advantages by choosing English or Scots law unless the trust otherwise qualifies as a Scottish or English trust.

RECOGNITION OF FOREIGN TRUSTS

One of the primary purposes of the Hague Convention was to provide for the recognition of trusts by legal systems that do not recognise trusts.

A fundamental problem for the drafters of the Convention was that the institution of trust is not recognised in many countries so the Convention simply could not state that these countries will recognise a "trust". Such a term would have been meaningless to those countries. Instead Art. 2 contains a lengthy list of the characteristics of a trust and these countries will recognise as a trust any entity which has these characteristics.

Consequences of recognition

If an institution with the characteristics outlined in Art. 2 is valid according to the applicable law, that institution will be recognised in all countries ratifying the Hague Convention whether or not these countries have trusts in their own domestic laws (Art. 11).

Recognition always means that the legal system of the ratifying country accepts three things:

(a) that the trust property constitutes a separate fund;
(b) that the trustee may sue and be sued in his capacity as trustee; and
(c) that the trustee may appear or act in this capacity before a notary or any person acting in an official capacity.

As well as the three mandatory consequences of recognition there are four other consequences of recognition which the legal system of the ratifying country accepts but only if the law applicable to the trust so provides. These are:

(a) that the personal creditors of the trustee shall have no recourse against the trust assets;
(b) that the trust assets shall not form part of the trustee's estate upon his insolvency or bankruptcy;
(c) that the trust assets shall not form part of the matrimonial property of the trustee or his spouse nor part of the trustee's estate on his death; and
(d) that the assets may be recovered when the trustee, in breach of trust, has mingled trust assets with his own property or has alienated trust assets. In such a case it is provided that the rights and obligations of any third party holder of the assets shall remain subject to the law determined by the choice of law rules of the forum (the place where a dispute is determined).

Exceptions to recognition

There are three exceptions to the recognition of a trust and the consequences of recognition. These are:

(1) Article 15 provides that if the recognition of a trust or any aspect of it would clash with a mandatory provision of the legal system governing the trust, according to the private international law rules of the forum (*i.e.* the choice of law rules which would have been applied if the Convention had not been ratified) then the mandatory provisions will be applied. This prevents a truster choosing a legal system to avoid Scottish rules to protect parties such as children, creditors in matters of insolvency, third parties acting in good faith and in respect of legal rights to protect disinheritance of family members such as *jus relictae* and legitim.

(2) Article 16 provides that if the recognition of a trust or any aspect of it would clash with a mandatory provision of the legal system of the forum then the mandatory provisions will be applied. This protects the interest of the state by preventing a truster from choosing a foreign legal system to avoid matters such as currency regulations or export restrictions.

(3) Article 18 allows for the provisions of the Convention to be disregarded where their application would be manifestly contrary to public policy.

APPENDIX: SAMPLE EXAMINATION QUESTIONS AND ANSWER PLANS

Question 1

Will D. Hughes and Bert Kilpatrick are trustees in respect of the mortis causa *trust set up by Harry Watt. Both trustees are first cousins of Harry Watt. The purposes of the trust are to provide monetary grants for any of Harry Watt's first and second cousins who are retired musicians residing within a 20 mile radius of Aberdeen, particularly those who have played highland bagpipes. The beneficiaries comprise a group of 20 people. When the trust was set up it was endowed with £100,000 cash by Harry Watt. In the trust deed the trustees were granted the "widest powers of investment" and given discretion to choose when to pay the beneficiaries within the class identified by the truster.*

Five years have elapsed since the commencement of the trust and Will D. Hughes has retired as a trustee. Although he signed a document of resignation, he never obtained a discharge in respect of his intromissions. He still lives in Aberdeen. Bert Kilpatrick asks David Dowling to be a new trustee and David accepts without further enquiry. David Dowling admits to Bert Kilpatrick that he knows nothing whatsoever about investment and tells Bert simply to continue the existing investment policy "whatever that is". David Dowling takes no steps to supervise Bert Kilpatrick and never queries what he is doing.

Six months later Bert Kilpatrick disappears.

David Dowling then decides to have the accounts of the trust audited and discovers the following:

(1) Except for £10,000, none of the trust funds had been invested except to place them in a Scottish bank account with a very low rate of return.

(2) £10,000 had been invested in shares in an Icelandic coal mining venture which has completely failed. No advice was taken in respect of this investment.

(3) When paying out various grants. Will D. Hughes and Bert Kilpatrick had awarded themselves grants of £20,000 each on the basis that they had been members of a school pipe band. Will D. Hughes' money has been dissipated but Bert invested his in a salmon fishing beat on the river Don, Aberdeenshire. This beat has been let out to tourists for £6,000 a year for the last three years and this sum (now totalling £18,000) remains untouched in Bert's bank account in Aberdeen. The value of the beat has risen and it is now worth £30,000 on the open market.

(4) £10,000 has been paid out to Bert Kilpatrick's wife and she has purchased a car. She claims not to know where the money came from. The car is still in existence and is parked in her garage in Aberdeen. It is now worth £5,000.

David Dowling has come to you for advice. Can he be sued by anyone? If so, what defences are available to him?

Suggested Answer

David is in some difficulty here and is liable to be sued by the beneficiaries of the trust.

Once he has accepted office, a trustee must act personally and cannot generally delegate his duties either to another trustee or a third party. This is the application of the maxim *delegatus non potest delegare*. The maxim is a presumption rather than a general rule and it may be rebutted in appropriate circumstances. Nevertheless, David Dowling has effectively delegated his responsibilities by telling Bert to continue the existing investment policy "whatever that is" and by taking no steps to supervise Bert Kilpatrick or query what he is doing.

As regards defences available to David Dowling, consider:

(1) Trusts (Scotland) Act 1921, s. 3(d) — Unless the contrary is expressed all trusts are held to include a provision that each trustee is to be liable only for his own acts and intromissions and is not to be liable for the acts and intromissions of co-trustees or for omissions. Under this subsection trustees have been held not to be liable for the acts and intromissions of their predecessors (*Mackenzie's Exr v. Thomson's Trs* (1965)). However, the subsection does not prevent a trustee being liable for the breaches of his fellow trustees if he himself commits a breach of his own duty to the trust. Thus, it will probably not be sufficient to provide a defence for David as he abnegated all responsibility and did not supervise the acts of his fellow trustees. Because the fellow trustees carried out a breach of trust, David may be liable for failure not to supervise.

Altrhough the provision states that a trustee will not be liable for omissions, provisions of the 1921 Act, s. 3(d) will absolve a trustee only where there is a clear duty to act.

(2) Trusts (Scotland) Act 1921, s. 32 — In terms of the 1921 Act, s. 32 the court may relieve a trustee from liability if he acted honestly and reasonably and it appears to the court that he ought fairly to be excused for the breach of trust. David Dowling must establish both honesty and reasonableness to be granted relief. If David has acted honestly but not reasonably relief will not be granted (see *Clark v. Clark's Trs* (1925)). In this case a trustee honestly left a sum of money on deposit receipt for two years instead of investing part of it in an annuity as the trust deed required. It was held that this was not a reasonable course of action since the result was that the annuity would be charged on the whole trust fund and not only on the part that ought to have been invested. Relief under the 1921 Act, s. 32 was refused. It is likely that David may be able to show he acted honestly but his lack of supervision will make it difficult for him to show he acted reasonably.

In relation to the various acts and omissions of the trustees the following points can be made:

(1) As regards the trust funds invested in a Scottish bank account with a very low rate of return this will amount to a breach of trust by the trustee making the investment. Where trust property includes money it is not sufficient for the trustee to select very safe investments which generate a minimal return as would be the case if he placed all the trust funds on deposit receipt for an extended period and did not exercise any judgment in relation to investment (*Melville v. Noble's Trs* (1896)). David Dowling did not make the investment himself but he did not take action to review the investment within a reasonable period after accepting office. In this latter respect he will probably be regarded in breach of trust.

(2) There is a breach of trust in relation to the £10,000 invested in shares in an Icelandic coal mining venture which has completely failed. Such an investment falls wholly outwith the type of investments authorised by the Trustee Investments Act 1961. Even if advice had been taken the investments would still not be authorised under this statute. David Dowling did not participate in the decision to invest but he should have taken steps to ascertain the position and withdraw the trust funds from the investment as soon as possible after his appointment as trustee.

(3) There is a breach of trust in relation to the grants of £20,000 paid to Will D. Hughes and Bert Kilpatrick. There is an obvious conflict of interest here and it is insufficient to elide that conflict to show that they had been members of a school pipe band. Where a trustee has a power to exercise discretion he must not exercise it in his own favour. For example, in *Inglis v. Inglis* (1983) the estate of a deceased included the tenant's interest in an agricultural lease. The executor was one of a class of people comprising the deceased's heir on intestacy. In terms of the Succession (Scotland) Act 1964 the tenant's part in the lease could be transferred to any one of these people but the executor chose to transfer the lease to himself. The transfer was reduced.

Will D. Hughes' money has been dissipated and cannot be recovered. As regards Bert's investment in a salmon fishing beat on the river Don, there is the possibility of tracing of the trust property. The salmon fishing and the income therefrom will be held in a constructive trust for the benefit of the trustees under the original trust. The beneficiaries can recover not only the £18,000 of income but also the capital value of the beat (now £30,000). Where a trustee uses his position to obtain property for himself the trustee becomes a constructive trustee of any property that he obtains as a result of the breach of trust and any profit or advantage that he derives from the breach. A good example is the case of *University of Aberdeen v. Town Council of Aberdeen* (1877). The Town Council of Aberdeen acted as trustees in a trust for the benefit of the professors of the University of Aberdeen. The trust property consisted of the lands of Torry. The Town Council wanted the lands for themselves and sold them secretly at an auction to themselves. They then obtained a lease from the Crown Estate of the salmon fishings *ex adverso* the lands of Torry. The salmon fishings were sub-let by the Council and a rent was received by the Council. When the University found out about the sale 80 years later they brought an action against the Town Council for breach of trust. It was held that a breach of trust had occurred and the Council were obliged to return not only the lands of Torry but also the income from the fishings. The latter is significant because at no time were the University ever owners or tenants of the fishings (but the Town Council would never have been in a position to obtain a lease of these fishings if they had not abused their position as trustee).

(4) It is likely that there is a breach of trust because of a conflict of interest in relation to the money granted to Bert's wife. The car will be held on a constructive trust and may be traced by the beneficiaries. The exceptional case seen in *Burrell v. Burrell's Trs* (1915) will not apply. In that case it was held that the purchase of shipping shares belonging to a trust estate by the wife of one of the trustees, on her own initiative, out of her separate estate and for an adequate consideration was valid. In this case Bert's wife has not purchased anything out of her own funds. She simply has received a gift from the trust.

Question 2

Geoffrey MacMaster wishes to set up a trust for various purposes and has consulted you as to whether this is possible.

Comment on the validity of the following trust purposes which Geoffrey suggests:

(1) He wishes the trustees to manage his existing farm for such purposes as they think fit.

(2) He wishes the trustees to give a sum of £100,000 to such charities as they think fit.

(3) Geoffrey has a collection of red telephone boxes in his back yard. They are nothing special as regards architectural merit but he wishes the

trustees to construct a museum to preserve them intact so that they can be exhibited to the public.

(4) He wishes the trustees to make a reasonable provision for his two loyal sheepdogs for the rest of their natural life.

(5) Geoffrey informs you that he has invested in property in South America. He wishes the trustees to hold a farm located in Argentina for the benefit of his nephews, Harry, Larry, Barry, Cary and Gary.

Suggested Answer

There are considerable difficulties with the trust purposes suggested by Geoffrey. They may be summarised as follows:

(1) An instruction to trustees to manage a farm for such purposes as they think fit is too vague and will be unenforceable. Authority for this may be found in cases such as *Sutherland's Trs v. Sutherland's Trs* (1893) where it was held that directions for distribution were void from uncertainty where they directed the trustees to distribute the trust assets "in such manner as they may think proper" and *Wood v. Wood's Exrx* (1995) where a will appointed an executrix and directed her to distribute the estate "as she knows I would wish it". This was held void from uncertainty and the estate fell into intestacy.

(2) The instruction to trustees to give a sum of £100,000 to such charities as they think fit may be valid. It has been held that a trust for "charities" or "charitable purposes" is sufficiently precise at least where trustees are appointed and given power to make the choice (see *Angus's Exrx v. Batchan's Trs* (1949)).

(3) The instruction in relation to the telephone boxes may be regarded as contrary to public policy. It is possible that the trust purpose is so extravagant and wasteful that it is wholly lacking in benefit to the community. Authority may be found in *Sutherland's Trs v. Verschoyle* (1968) where a truster purported to set up a trust to display what she believed was a valuable art collection. The collection had little artistic value and the court held the purpose to be void on the basis that it was completely wasteful and contrary to public policy.

(4) The trust purpose to provide a reasonable provision for the sheepdogs is valid. Although this sort of trust purpose may appear to run contrary to the principle that a trust purpose is valid only if it confers some beneficial interest in property on another living person, an exception is made for animals. According to one method of analysis, in such cases the beneficiaries are not the animals but the general public. The purpose of the trust for animals may be regarded as the welfare of animals but it is the public in general who receive the benefit of having the animals looked after.

(5) A trust of foreign land is invalid if the legal system where the land is situated does not give effect to trusts (*Brown's Trs v. Gregson* (1920)). In that case a testator who was domiciled in Scotland conveyed his whole estate (including immoveable property in Argentina) to trustees in trust for children. By Argentine law, trusts were not recognised or given effect. The

settlement was declared null as regards the Argentine property by the Argentine courts and this Argentine decision was recognised by Scots law.

Question 3

Billy Brown is the sole trustee in a trust set up for the purpose of holding property for a partnership of architects. The partnership assets comprise the exclusive property right in an office in Aberdeen. He is getting on in years and is worried about his health. He has been told by his friend in the pub that he should make suitable provision in a will and he has come to you for advice. He instructs you to leave the property to his son so that the son can continue to be the trustee.

You check the trust deed and it contains no express power on the part of the trustees to assume new trustees. Give suitable advice to Billy.

Suggested Answer

(1) Although the real right of property in trust property rests with Billy as trustee and he may be considered the owner of the trust property (*per* Lord Moncrieff in *Inland Revenue v. Clark's Trs* (1939)), Billy's right to the property is constrained by the right of the beneficiaries. Billy cannot use the trust property for his own purposes as if it were his own property. He may not leave it in a will to his son.

(2) As a sole trustee, Billy's power to resign is constrained. In terms of the Trusts (Scotland) Act 1921, s. 3(a) and proviso (1) a sole trustee cannot resign his office unless he has assumed "new trustees" who have accepted office, or the court has appointed new trustees or a judicial factor. The section is badly worded and it is possible to argue that because the statute refers to "new trustees" (plural) a sole trustee must appoint more than one trustee before he can resign. In *Kennedy, Ptr* (1983) this argument was rejected and a sole executrix was permitted to resign when she appointed a single executor to act in her place.

(3) There are other difficulties arising because Billy is a sole trustee. If Billy dies in office he will cease to be a trustee and his executors will not automatically become trustee in his place. There will be difficulties if no new trustees are appointed before Billy dies. The title to the trust estate will remain in the deceased sole trustee and will require to be taken out of his name by a process of conveyancing. A statutory procedure is set out in the Trusts (Scotland) Act 1921, ss. 22 and 24. There is an alternative procedure which will allow Billy's executor to add the trust property into the inventory attached to his confirmation and thus obtain judicial sanction to transfer the trust property to a person who may be legally authorised to continue the administration of the trust estate or, alternatively, direct to the beneficiaries if the administration is complete (see the Executors (Scotland) Act 1900, s. 6 as amended by the Succession (Scotland) Act 1964, ss. 14(1), 34(1) and Sched. 2, para. 3).

(4) Billy should consider appointing new trustees now. Although the trust deed contains no express power of appointment this should not be a

problem. New trustees may be assumed by an existing trustee unless this power is expressly excluded by the trust deed (Trusts (Scotland) Act 1921, s. 3(b)). There is no such express exclusion here.

(5) Billy may wish to consider the appointment of a corporate trustee. One benefit of a corporate trustee is that it never dies and thus avoids the difficulties in relation to continuity of administration which arise where a natural person dies and that person is a sole trustee. In *Leith's Exr* (1937) this benefit was a factor in the appointment of a new trustee by the court under the Trusts (Scotland) Act 1921, s. 22. Where limited companies are incorporated for the purpose of being a trustee or executor it is likely that they will have specialised provisions in the objects clause of their memorandum of association.

Question 4

Annie MacIvor, Alice McKeefry, Bill Benson, Louis Tone and Sammy Smith are appointed as trustees in a mortis causa *deed of trust granted by Alex McKeefry. The trust estate consists of £300,000 in cash. The purpose of the trust is to provide grants to ten of Alex's indigent relatives living in Stonehaven. There are no special qualifications for trustees set out in the trust deed. Alex has now died and the first four potential trustees turn up at your office. You also receive a telephone call from Jimmy Smith (son of Sammy Smith) confirming that Sammy Smith has died but that Jimmy Smith would be willing to act as trustee. Upon further enquiry you become aware of the following points:*

(1) Annie MacIvor is aged 10;

(2) Alice McKeefry is resident in Australia and is not a British citizen;

(3) Bill Benson suffers occasionally from depression and, from time to time, requires to be admitted to hospital for treatment;

(4) Louis Tone is an undischarged bankrupt and has been convicted for fraud on three occasions; and

(5) Jimmy Smith is entirely reliable and is of full age. He would make an ideal trustee.

Suggested Answer

Generally speaking any person who has the legal capacity to hold and deal with property is qualified to act as a trustee but there are a number of problems here.

(1) Annie MacIver is too young to be a trustee. A person under 16 cannot be a trustee (see the Age of Legal Capacity (Scotland) Act 1985, s. 1(1) and s. 9(5)). The existing trustees may be able to assume her as a trustee when she reaches that age.

(2) The fact that Alice McKeefry is not a British citizen does not disqualify her from being a trustee. None of the special rules relative to ships or aircraft have any relevance because the trust property comprises cash

only (see, *e.g.* Air Navigation Order 1989 (S.I. 1989 No. 2004), as amended by subsequent regulations).

Alice's residence abroad is no bar to becoming a trustee, although by statute it is made a ground on which, in certain circumstances, the court may remove a trustee (1921 Act, s. 23). With modern facilities for travel and communication such residence must cause less inconvenience than in former times.

(3) Bill Benson's illness is no reason for his not being appointed as trustee. An insane person cannot accept office as a trustee but depression does not amount to insanity. Not all forms of mental illness amount to insanity. Only if the illness is sufficiently severe to prevent an understanding of the powers, duties and responsibilities of the office of trusteeship will this be sufficient to exclude a party from being a trustee. The issue of insanity more often arises as a ground for removal of a trustee from office.

The Trusts (Scotland) Act 1921, s. 23 also permits removal on the grounds of "incapacity through mental ... disability". This may permit removal of a trustee who suffers from psychiatric illness or weakness which falls short of insanity provided it is sufficient to impair materially the trustee's ability to carry out his function.

(4) Louis Tone's character may give rise to some doubts but he is not automatically disqualified from the office of trustee. An insolvent party (even if he has been sequestrated) is not generally disqualified from being a trustee. This is not a charitable trust where there are special rules to disqualify insolvent parties (Law Reform (Miscellaneous Provisions) (Scotland) Act 1990, s. 8). Secondly, the convictions for fraud are no grounds for disqualification at common law. In charitable trusts there are special rules to disqualify those convicted of crimes involving dishonesty (but this is not relevant here given the nature of the trust) (Law Reform (Miscellaneous Provisions) (Scotland) Act 1990, s. 8). Nevertheless, if Louis Tone is a disreputable character this could bode ill for the administration of the trust. If he continues in his criminal ways and is incarcerated with the result that he becomes incapable of performing his duties as a trustee this may be founded upon as a ground for removal of a trustee.

(5) Jimmy Smith cannot become a trustee just because his father was appointed as trustee. There is a strong element of *delectus personae* in relation to the choice of trustees. Nevertheless, given the good character of Jimmy, it would be prudent to see if the other trustees would exercise their powers to assume Jimmy as a trustee in terms of the Trusts (Scotland) Act 1921, s. 3(b)). As an adviser, you cannot force the existing trustees to exercise this power.

INDEX

103